THE GREEN MOVEMENT IN IRAN

THE GREEN MOVEMENT IN IRAN

Hamid Dabashi

Edited with an introduction by
Navid Nikzadfar

Transaction Publishers
New Brunswick (U.S.A.) and London (U.K.)

Library of Congress Catalog Number: 2011000419
ISBN: 978-1-4128-1841-4
Printed in the United States of America

Library of Congress Cataloging-in-Publication Data

Dabashi, Hamid, 1951-
    The green movement in Iran / Hamid Dabashi.
        p. cm.
    ISBN 978-1-4128-1841-4
        1. Green movement--Iran 2. Social movements--Iran. 3. Social change--Iran. 4. Presidents--Iran--Election--2009. 5. Elections--Iran. 6. Iran--Politics and government--1997- I. Title.

JA75.8.D33 2011
320.5'80955--dc22

                                                                    2011000419

Contents

Preface   vii

Introduction   1

1   Highlights of the Events   23

2   The Nature and Political Consequences
     of the Green Movement   43

3   The Green Movement and Iran's Contemporary
     Political History   73

4   Legitimacy Challenges to the "Islamic Republic"   81

5   Responses to the "Left" and Other Accounts
     of the Situation   97

6   US Politics, Iran, and the Green Movement   123

7   The Green Movement, the Palestinian Cause,
     and Racism   153

8   Islamic Republic Tactics in Staging Legitimacy   161

Preface

Yar-e dabestani-ye man/ba man-o hamrah-e mani (*Oh my schoolmate/ You are my friend and comrade*) ... It was late in June 2009, soon after the commencement of the Green Movement in Iran, when my wife Golbarg Bashi and I had joined a vigil in Union Square in New York, when suddenly the younger members of the gathering burst into this beautiful song, whose lyrics and melody I did not know—and it bothered me that I did not know. I subsequently researched the song and through my wife's connections found the composer in Sweden and learned everything about the origin of the song and why, how, and when it had become the unofficial anthem of the younger generation of student activists.

That early lesson in humility became a telling example for me that I needed to be exceedingly cautious in how and in what particular terms I was to understand the Green Movement. My surest bet was to trust its signs, learn its songs and symbols, and follow its indexical leads where they led me. Based on these, and everything else I knew and learned, and from the very commencement of the Green Movement in Iran in June 2009, I decided, almost instantly, to consider and understand it as a *civil rights movement* and not as a *revolution*. This was a conscious and deliberate choice based on how I thought the movement had originated and where it was headed. But from the very beginning, I was also very cognizant of a major generational gap that was separating me from some 80% of other Iranians who are under the age of 40. This awareness made me very cautious in my observations, judicious in my reading of the event, and yet purposeful in all I said and suggested about the Green Movement.

This collection of essays you are about to read carries the instantaneous signs of trying to come to terms with an unfolding civil rights movement as it is in progress. This is for the second time in my life, a major social uprising in my homeland has sent me back to the drawing board—earlier, when the Iranian Revolution of 1977–1979 happened, and later, in mid-2009 when the Green Movement started. There is something exciting and vertiginous to try to see the contours of a movement of whose precise direction only the future generations can speak with ease and confidence. I like the creative unease and the spontaneity and urgency of the prose with which I have written these essays, some of which I have subsequently reworked in my other publications for a more sustained and purposeful analytical framing and theoretical purpose.

Navid Nikzadfar is a pseudonym for a young Iranian social scientist I have come to know and admire, and who is the person who has edited this volume and written a learned introduction to it. We became acquainted when he wrote me an e-mail, back in July 2009, soon after he had read a piece I had just written on the Green Movement. This acquaintance soon grew in detecting a common strand of theoretical and political thrust, hooked together from two generations of Iranian social thinkers with, if not common then, complementary points of view. Soon I invited Navid to start looking at all my writings on the Green Movement, in both Persian and English, with a view toward making his own selection of them, giving them the order and trajectory he thought best, and writing an introduction to the whole collection. This I thought, and he concurred, would tantamount to a fictive but enduring handshake across two generations so that I give him all I have and he pushes them forward and moves on, for whatever I am worth, and for whatever he can make of me on this seminal event in our homeland.

That he has opted to remain anonymous is his choice, with the necessity of a life lived between home and abroad. He is afraid that there might (and there will) be adverse consequences for him if he were to publish what he has written in his introduction under his own name and signature. I categorically disagree with and disapprove of pseudonyms. But I respect and honor his choice and decision and perfectly understand it. I am confident that he will one day come out and publish groundbreaking work of his own and under his own real name and signature. That day, which I hope and trust is not too distant, he may even opt to come back and claim what is his: This "Introduction"—his signature nod that I am not too off the mark in thinking what I have thought, in these pages, which he has woven together for you to read and think through whatever it is that is happening in our homeland.

Hamid Dabashi
New York, January 2011

Introduction

Contemporary Political History of Iran:
Struggle for Independence and Democracy

Contemporary political history of Iran can simply be summarized in terms of a continuous struggle for (true) independence and ambitions for political development and democracy at various levels. The history of Iran has witnessed prolonged pseudocolonization and puppet rulers, while the foreign powers' influences in Iranian affairs were the order of the day. The ideal of independence and democratic governance have been carved in the political psyche of the nation historically and more vividly in the past 100 years. Though never *officially* colonized, the Iranian state has long been subservient to colonial powers, switching from one to another or two at the same time, in which periods the monarchial state would give economic and political concessions to all parties to save the throne. Consequently, Iran has constantly been a site of colonial rivalry. The monarchs and governments were either practically "big-boys" elements in power or had substantial allegiance to them, as their reigns had generally no democratic legitimacy and/or efficiency for that matter. As such, the two major recurrent ideals of democratic development and independence have always been (and are) complementary factors for an Iranian context.

Iran's historical struggle for the establishment of an accountable modern government can be traced back to 200 years.[1] However, the Constitutional Revolution (1907–1911) as a first-of-the-kind phenomenon in the region was a remarkable manifestation of these aspirations which influenced the Iranian polity in important ways. The Constitutional Revolution was an influential attempt to establish a publicly legitimated system of governance in contrast to the traditional monarchial "God-given" legitimacy. Although the developments before and after the Constitutional Revolution marked a

1

bright period in the contemporary history of Iran and paved the way for several other developmental stages, domestic issues, for example, the low level of literacy, the historical despotic orientations, along with the practical objection of the influential colonial power of the time, that is, Russia, hindered the establishment of a sustainable system of democratic governance.

In the nineteen and early twentieth century, the then powerful northern neighbor of Iran, Russia, and the ubiquitous and powerful British Empire had widespread and determining influence in Iran—obviously a negative effect on Iran's political development. The Constitutional Revolution in the first decade of the twentieth century was initially foiled by direct Russian interference which fiercely opposed the constitutional aspirations of the revolution. Russians indiscreetly attacked the constitutionalists, gave political, military, and logistic support to Mohammad Ali Shah to conduct his notorious campaign against constitutionalism, for example, shelling of the first democratic parliament of Iran, killing the first popularly elected Members of Parliament (MPS) and the subsequent intimidations, executions, and imprisonment of constitutionalist intellectuals and politicians.

In the meantime, the British Empire enjoyed prolonged and vast influence in Iran with more concentration in the central and southern parts. It is no surprise that the two powers, the British and the Russians, practically signed contracts—between themselves—to divide Iran into two interest zones on two separate occasions.

By the time Reza Shah was installed as the first Pahlavi Shah of Iran in 1925, the influence of the British was generally outweighing that of the Russians, while the United States was emerging as the new global superpower, jostling its position in oil-rich Iran. The internal weakness and lack of popular legitimacy of the ruling authorities in Iran resurfaced, once again, when Reza Shah was forced to abdicate by the Anglo-Russian invasion of Iran in 1941. Less than a decade following the installation of Mohammad Reza Shah, the son of Reza Shah, as the second Pahlavi king, there came about another major popular uprising for similar ideals of independence and democratic government in Iran, led by the popularly supported Mossadegh. Mossadegh, who was anticolonial, nationalized the Iranian oil industry, stripping it off the control of the British, and launched a series of social and political reforms to return to the Constitutional Revolution's ideas, including restricting the role of the Shah to a ceremonial position. Yet, the cycle of domestic inefficiencies, foreign interference, and the lack of a well-established grassroot civil society repeated itself with the poignantly notorious Anglo-American coup against Mossadegh's government in 1953, which left a scar on the political psyche of Iranians. The coup mortified the nation in their historical powerlessness and subsequently, in less than a decade, gave way to a religiously indoctrinated struggle for independence and freedom in Iran as more violent strategies for struggle against the Shah's bandwagon dictatorial reign were adopted.

Toppling Mossadegh and reinstalling Mohammad Reza Shah, in 1953, who had already fled the country with the escort of the British/ American intelligence was perhaps the most ostentatious reminder for Iranians of the old wounds and marked the year 1953 as the beginning of a new era during which the application of religion as a tool for anticolonial and antidictatorial struggles started to become more important, as the role of the United States in Iranian affairs was dramatically increasing.

Soon the Shah's government—backed by the United States and major Western powers—engaged in a full-swing operation of suppressing dissidence of any kind. In the meantime, Iran's historical aspirations were being theorized, this time by drawing on a newly interpreted revolutionary Islamic discourse. Noncleric public intellectuals such as Ali Shariati and Jalal Al-e Ahmad, as well as clerics such as Ayatollah Khomeini and Ayatollah Motahari, among several others, contributed to such Islamic revolutionary discourse.[2]

Iran's Islamic Revolution of 1979 can, therefore, be viewed as yet another attempt against dictatorship, authoritarianism, and foreign powers' interference in Iran. Ayatollah Khomeini, who soon became the undisputed leader of the Revolution, voiced similar emancipatory and progressive goals for the Islamic Revolution—although in a recurrent religious tone—and turned himself into a leader for almost all groups who were anticolonial, antiauthoritarian, and pro-democracy, rather than a purely religious leader.[3] Several political trends and major parties, armed and unarmed, contributed to the 1979 Iran Revolution, including the secular, anticolonial, pro-democracy groups and left-leaning socialist groups and religious groups, as well as what can be classified in between these three major groups.[4]

In practice, despite their apparent and most celebrated success in axing the continuum of foreign powers' interference in Iran, the custodians of the Islamic Republic of Iran gradually and violently removed all the "other" tendencies and turned the system into a solely

Islamic one. While the establishment of the Islamic Republic and monopolization of the political power involved major violent and socially traumatic events, including thousands of executions, several major bombings and assassinations, the suppressive, authoritarian nature of the Islamic Republic of Iran became more publicly apparent, first, after the end of the Iran–Iraq War in 1989 and, specifically in mid-1990, the reformist government of Khatami in 1997 and the subsequent developments.

The Islamic Republic of Iran and Its Oppositions

The Islamic Republic crushed the cosmopolitan and diverse political culture of Iran and enforced a top-down Islamization of various fields, for example, education, political participations, etc. To strip the nation of its colorful political plurality, the regime has been systematically exploiting the anticolonial aspirations of the Iranians which could only be framed within a political Islamic culture. As such, it has been constructing and pursuing a discourse of strict dichotomies, including Islamic Republic or colonial dependence, Political Islamic or blind, shallow Westernism, and Islamic Republic or the old Shah's reign.

In the spring of 2009, the Islamic Republic of Iran seemed quite settled in its geopolitical, ideological, regional, and international power. Exploiting the troublesome global political context, the Islamic Republic administered by an increasing tyrannical control domestically, contingent upon—real and/or constructed—imperial overtones of the West. Its contented reign systematically tapped into and benefited from the construction of the homogenous, essentialist evil of the "other," that is, the United States/West, while being preoccupied with destroying the last shreds of rationality through demagoguery and the divisionist lumpanism of Ahmadinejad.

What the regime overlooked was the (re)budding culture of cosmopolitanism among the remarkably young population of Iran, which had started showing symptoms of resentment for not only the long lasting, over-ideologicalization of their otherwise pluralist society but also for the over-dichotomization of their world into parades of binaries: the imperial United States versus Islamic Iran, the colonial West versus the revolutionary Iran, the malfunctioning, tyrannical Islamic Republic versus a cluster of its old malfunctioning, inarticulate expatriate opposition groups, for example, the Monarchist, Mujahedin Khalgh Iran.

The wave of sociopolitical change had already surfaced as the tip of the iceberg in domestic underground music within the last decade, with the recent outburst of a strong, organic, generally angry, and highly critical, rap and hip-hop music from within Iran. Despite various legal restrictions and risks for recording, playing, and distributing of such underground music, the popularity and strengths of this organic turn was so compelling that, in fact, pushed—to some extent—its style, lyrics, and overtones onto the Persian music industry in Los Angeles. Such a general turn in music with its usually angry and critical lyrics did not only target the social and political issues of the society but attempted to anchor and restore the space centrality *inside* Iran and challenge the projected high ground of the mainstream Persian diaspora music Mecca, that is, Los Angeles.

Similar trends could be seen amid the bulk of the Iranian diaspora in gradually rejecting the constructed debilitating dichotomous standoffs which would, for example, automatically and monolithically transform any political dissent inside or outside the country into a support for Monarchist (supporting the prerevolutionary "secular" Shah) or other old opposition groups and—in equally brutal essentialist ways—brand any other tendency as a staunch supporter of the Islamic Republic. A dichotomy, which presented to Iranians both inside and outside, an *either-or* choice, between—in Dabashi's terms—a "colonial modernity" and an equally retrograde anticolonial traditionalism in a way that both choices would entail high ideological enmity toward one another with consequences of bifurcation of Iran into traditional versus modern, secular versus religious, Western versus traditional, uptown "cultured" middle class versus downtown cultureless poor, Tehrani versus provincial, and the like.

Smoldered within a visionary stagnation of a constructed duality in swinging between an increasingly suppressive regime of the Islamic Republic and the feeble, misinformed alternatives of the mainstream Iranian exile oppositions—deliberately and strategically orchestrated and promoted by the Islamic Republic and blindly pursued by the Other—the Iranian thriving society had found itself at a loss for a visionary and viable solution for the future.

Nevertheless, such strategic dichotomization, that is, the reactionary aspirations of the increasingly disconnected, hawkish opposition in the United States on the one hand, and the siding with, or remaining silent about, the blatant authoritarian, oppressive Islamic Republic on the other hand, ceased to function all of a sudden and provided the defining features for the emergence of a strong endogenous uprising which not only opposed steadfastly the decades of suppression, manipulation, lies, and delusional reductionist Islamization of the highly diversified Iranian nation but also left behind the inarticulate, retrograde ideals of opposition groups in exile.

The old, exile oppositions of the Islamic Republic had very little to offer for the future. On the one hand, it was the psychologically crippling (yet, legitimate) grudges of these opposition groups against the Islamic Republic, as the product of the 1979 revolution had long prevented them from healthy critical debates internally and externally, and on the other hand, such an approach had blurred their political narratives retrospectively in terms of the Iranian contemporary political history resulting in an ideological and backward reading of the postrevolutionary events. The Iranian expatriate opposition groups' projected alternatives are highly antagonistic, but never profoundly theorized, and often constructed rudimentarily in terms of whatever the Islamic Republic *is not*. The hawkish—and to a lesser extent now, ubiquitous—dominant dichotomization of good and evil in public and political discourses of the United States at the same time did little but to reinforce such simplified Manichean worldviews and, hence, contributed (and is contributing) to the theoretical and practical dead end in providing a realistic, organic account of events and possible solutions.

Iran's Postrevolutionary Account

The sociopolitical discontinuity and lack of "life world" experiences in terms of the events on the ground in Iran during the past 30 years of the revolution—when the main bulk of the opposition was forced to go on exile between 1979 and 1981—and the adoption of an inaccurate narrative of the contemporary political history of Iran have contributed heavily to various misinformed accounts of Iran not only by the dominant discourses of the Iranian exile groups but also among some international observers including the "left" intellectuals. As such, 30 years of dramatic and significant events in Iran imprinted on the political psyche of the nation are either deliberately or carelessly ignored in these accounts. Similarly, in American public discourses, many accounts of Iran jump from the "hostage taking crisis" in the period 1979–1981 to Iran's nuclear challenges after Ahmadinejad assumed power in 2005, overlooking major events and ideological/discursive changes in the characteristics of the nation.

Iran as it stands now—in addition to its rich prerevolutionary and historical background—is a nation deeply influenced and shaped by various trajectories. Among these are the political chaos, insecurity

6

and bloodshed of the early years of the revolution, the long and full-fledged war (1981–1989) with Iraq with its ideological/psychological consequences, for example, mobilization of almost all layers of the society to defend and fight for the country; economic consequences, for example, widespread rationing and scarcity of basic food and services, long queues, state-administered industry, services; and sociopsychological consequences, for example, life under emergency status, life in underground shelters, ideologicalization of education, and an inherited "normalcy" in emergency, which would take the omnipresent violence as given for the new generation.

After the war ended in 1989, the society aspired to take a deep breath to take a look around but not through the lens of war and ideology. This was followed by the announcement of the economic reforms agenda which, in turn, brought about a sudden and new thirst and greed for socioeconomic status in contrast to the heroic spirit of the war—as corruption skyrocketed through the abuse of various social, religious, institutional, and political power sources and led to a sudden growth of a new but familiar clientalist culture which fitted itself surreptitiously into the stated policies of privatization.

Khatami's sociopolitical reforms in 1997 called for a more vibrant public sphere and a "normal" life amid the increasing awareness in the general public about the contradictory political nature of the Islamic Republic system. Some acute criticism in academic and intellectual circles prompted debates on the nature and ideals of the Islamic Republic among intellectuals/students and, to a lesser degree, the general public. Before the turn of the millennium, the theoretically mobilized elites' demands for political reforms surpassed that of what Khatami's reformist government could or was ready to provide and this in turn led to the 1999 student uprising. The student uprising of 1999 was the first open public challenge to the legitimacy of the Islamic Republic, since it had managed to totalize the political scene after the 1979 revolution. The anticlimax of the clamp-down on students and the historic series of press closures gave rise to the excommunication of the reformers in power by some reference groups, for example, students and intellectuals, and there came about a political confusion as well as an increasing political apathy among the influential groups, for example, students, during the years leading to Ahmadinejad's election in 2005.

On the economic domain, the continued economic dissatisfaction, the day-to-day pressures, the endless struggle to make ends meet for large groups of the general public, the economic insecurity, nightmarish inflation, and the insatiable greed to exploit on the side of the clique with links to (economic, religious, and political) power had already created a new overnight bureaucratic (upper) middle class which had fierce ideo-logical/political/military allegiance to the rulers amid the reprimanding gaze of a dormant and economically aggrieved population.

In the 2005 presidential election, Ahmadinejad heavily focused his campaign—almost exclusively—on economic, anticorruption, and anticlientalist promises and managed to convince some sections of the society of having genuine aspirations, while most reference political groups, along with major parts of society, were bewildered and/or apathetic with general disappointment. Soon after the election, Ahmadinejad re-ideologicalized the Iranian domestic and foreign policies under a strategic conflation of socioeconomic gaps and ideo-logical confrontations internally and internationally. On the one hand, he exploited the dissatisfaction of large lower and/or marginalized sections of the society by his ad hoc distribution of cash, and on the other hand, redefined and reintroduced the sources of *all* economic and political problems within the old ideological standoff against the constructed Other, that is, the United States/West.

The Iranian society on the verge of the June 2009 presidential election carried a heavy baggage of various wounds and unfulfilled promises. From major issues regarding democratic political develop-ment, for example, lack of accountability for power, lack of freedom of speech and press, oxymoron political structure, and the continued top-down Islamization of the Iranian pluralistic society to—strongly related but different in focus—economic dissatisfaction, for example, high unemployment, lack of long-term and clear economic models and back-breaking inflation to sociocultural malignancies such as a lack of functional social ethics, lack of fair distribution of wealth and opportunities, discrimination, and clientalist.

As such, a realistic account of the Iranian affair turns into an es-sentially complicated one. Any unhealthy reductionist approach in dealing with Iran—be it in the form of lack of clear understanding of its contemporary political history or attempts in top-down imposi-tion of an existing (Western/Eastern) theory or analytical framework without regard to the immediate context—would be doomed to be irrelevant, if not detrimental, to the future of Iran.

It is important to note that on the verge of the June 2009 presidential election, none of the grievances of Iranian society mentioned above was derived from any larger-than-life ideology. In fact, the highly creative society of Iran, as it stands now, is weary of ideology and appears to favor life demands of all sorts: economic stability and security, social/cultural justice, political development, social freedom, freedom of speech, freedom of press, and cultural plurality. Such demands that call for a free and better life come from a nation that is historically sensitive to, and traumatized by, powerlessness and injustice; a society that is weary of over ideologicalization and social engineering, which is weary of constant turmoil; and a never-ending emergency status demanding sacrifice, for example, giving up domestic development for delusional confrontation with the "enemy," if not lives.

A society which is weary of 30 years of ideological militarization against this and that, weary of violence, either of the kind where bombs that—then internationally supported—Saddam was dropping on civilians in cities for years, or the violent invasion of privacy carried out by plainclothes *Basijis* at their random road blocks in the heart of the city—in a nutshell, a society that resents political, economic and social violence, and insecurity and desires to add to its independence the right and power to seek solace and empowerment without having to deal with ideological tantrums.

June 2009 Election and the Iranian Green Movement

Four years of Ahmadinejad's governance showed to most of this deeply violence-stricken and already frustrated society that there is always room for worse. At the time of elections in June 2009, this worsened situation was perhaps more obvious and relevant to more educated sections of society compared to the rural population, which may have thought of Ahmadinejad as a down-to-earth politician with genuine aspirations to implement fair economic reforms. The election abruptly flipped a large majority of the already quiet, frustrated Iranians into a euphoric, outspoken mood, as there was a sudden realization of the opportunity to bring about change—as small as it might be—through the most civil, nonviolent mechanism of voting. As such, the nation erupted with the most vibrant election campaigns in its history.

Iran's presidential election on June 12, 2009, and indeed months leading up to it, witnessed a sudden outcry from previously officially silent (and/or silenced) Iranians, who filled the social and political atmosphere of Iran with hope, empowerment, confidence, and euphoria in what could be seen as not only a mere option for change but also a chance to avoid falling for any either-or bifurcation. The unrivaled mobilization of the public throughout Iran and the general spirit of respect for each other, regardless of political allegiance, brought about the hope of change beyond merely removing the demagogue. Weeks before the election day, Tehran and many other major cities had a routine of nightly public gatherings and debates in which the overt and overwhelming majority of non-Ahmadinejad supporters (supporters of Mousavi and Karroubi) were cheerfully campaigning for their candidates and celebrating with a few supporters of Ahmadinejad on motorbikes or cars. There were even scenes of celebration in which supporters of all candidates were joining together. The euphoria was not just for *the change* itself but perhaps, more importantly, for the perceived actual *possibility for change*. June 12, 2009 was a historic day for Iran; there was such unity among all groups of Iranians that one could not have believed that there had been various social dichotomies in the previous year—they seemed to have vanished. Voting turned into a national struggle for Iran, for its future, for *our* country, and not necessarily for an election held by the Islamic Republic.

Before the official voting time was over, the smiles started to vanish from people's faces and various signs of an antieuphoric interference became apparent. In less than 2 hours after the ballot stations were officially closed, to the shock of millions of Iranians, it was announced that Ahmadinejad was leading with 70% of the votes. In less than 24 hours, Ahmadinejad was declared winner, achieving a landslide victory; and as the supreme leader he had also issued his confirmation of the results and thanked the Interior Ministry for carrying out an "impeccable historic election" and the Iranian nation for its "support of the Islamic Republic."

The preelection euphoric confidence soon—after being temporarily overwhelmed—turned into fury and defiance. What followed may have appeared to some as a popular movement for claiming back a subverted election; however, it was the *actual* start of an unpredicted massive protest movement, the aspirations, endurance, and scale of which caught almost all the observers off-guard. Everybody, from analysts and public intellectuals inside Iran to all expatriate opposition groups down to the core of the custodians of the Islamic Republic and its intelligence strategists were exposed to a sudden burst of highly politicalized masses that were, up until the election, considered to have been strongly apathetic to politics and/or were crushed and silenced by the theoretical dichotomy of the two evils.

The unprecedented mobilization of Iranians in the June 2009 election was, in effect, the result of the strong desire of a generally subjugated society that sought a peaceful change—even if it was as little as merely replacing Ahmadinejad with a reformist candidate. Iranian society was then a generally powerless nation which seemed to have fallen in love with ballot boxes as a viable means of showing protest without risking their lives and facing violence. The June 2009 election was a rather desperate attempt of a violence-stricken nation to consent to (perhaps) a minimum change. An attempt to reclaim the power to influence the political structure and nudge it to a more rational path without having to turn to violence.

While the heads of known Iranian opposition groups in exile had boycotted the election, as it would have legitimized the regime, and while the Western international media were obsessing with and reducing Iran to its nuclear program and Ahmadinejad, the Iranian nation turned out in epic millions in a hope for change.

The rise of an organic, homegrown opposition from within Iran broke through the visionary blockage created and strategically perpetuated by the choice between the debilitating opposite poles by a mass participation of the grassroot population inside Iran who not only sternly demanded a radical change in the Iranian polity but also left behind, in important ontological ways, the ideals of the exiled opposition groups. The Green Movement derives from and aims at a visionary future which is built on awareness and inclusion of 30 years of postrevolutionary realities and looks into the future as a step forward. The Green Movement has developed beyond the cult of personalities and seeks to install a strictly harnessed political power structure that serves the desires, ideals, and demands of the whole nation in its plurality. It is fiercely aware of its independence and demands to add a system of checks and balances, accountability, and the rule of law in all aspects of the Iranian political system.

The Iranian Green Movement includes a variety of political and social aspirations without being reduced to any of them . Although, at its onset, it has had a more middle class urban base, in its essence and political derives, it is (and increasingly becoming) a supraclass movement. It has supporters and activists who are secularists as well as Muslims, and socialists as well as nationalists; in a nutshell, it reflects what the cosmopolitan nature of the Iranian society actually *is*, rather than prescriptive approaches of what it (ideologically) *should* be. The Green Movement prioritizes democracy, plurality, and a vibrant public sphere over Islamism or Secularism. It transcends the politics of reductionist ideologies of Islamism or Secularism and concentrates on *rights and citizenry,* hence its central slogan of "Where is my vote."

To many, the eruption of mass street protests appears to be an impulsive explosion of collective dissent against a tainted election per se; nevertheless, the fact is that the Green Movement is a natural consequence of an epistemic change in postrevolutionary Iranian society—a society with two major experiences of secular and Islamist authoritarianism which is increasingly turning into a post-Islamist, postideological pluralist society. This is a society that prioritizes life over death and yet it recalcitrant against suppression, humiliation, and powerlessness. It is a movement for restoring power back to the people—whoever they are and whatever their aspirations may be. The Iranian Green Movement is the people's suppressed demands and an uprising against prescriptive and belittling attitudes of the rulers—Islamic or secular—who treat the people not as citizens with rights and demands but as naïve, gullible, and immature subjects who are incapable of having independent visions.

As Dabashi marks the end to Islamic ideology in Iran in 2000[5] and picks up a shift in the Iranian social psyche, the Green Movement, intellectually self-aware or experientially intuitive, is a struggle for actualizing "a dream that is neither Islamist nor Western, neither nativist nor 'Westoxicated,' and neither religious nor secular."[6] Similarly, as Dabashi argues in another article, "because of its prioritizing the civil rights demands, the Green Movement is a transideological and as such it marks the development of our political culture from 'political modernity' to 'social modernity.'"[7]

On the other hand, the Iranian society, as it stands now, is complicated and traumatized. It would only make sense to talk about Iranian society from within its own day-to-day context and/or from the angle of its historical and social problems. The Iranian society, and to some extent the Green Movement, suffers from real or fabricated, debilitating, if not fatal, bifurcations. The popular slogan of the Green Movement "we are all together" may need to permeate into deeper layers and in more diverse directions.

The custodians of the Islamic Republic in general and Ahmadinejad in particular have invested greatly and strategically in exploiting various fault lines in the society among social, religious, and political lines, for example, uptown affluent and downtown poor, and religious tendencies of devout groups and less religious (or secular) sections of society. Although, such divisions that roughly fall into the classic line of traditional versus modern have been heavily propagated and perpetuated by the Pahlavi regimes as well, the radical conservative populist government of Ahmadinejad has ardently tried to tap into such social gaps by parading these perceived dichotomies against each other. To exploit the historical, social, political, and economic subjugation of the urban poor and rural residents Ahmadinejad's administration has devised topicalization of banal, vulgar, and populist challenges as well as financial handouts to (legitimately) aggrieved lower classes. "We are all together" may need to watch out for such strategically devised and promoted discourse.

The same holds for all the other culturally normalized discriminatory classifications Other creating processes in the Iranians day-to-day conduct and discourses as well as those of political parties. More or less related to the core religious versus secular, rich versus poor in-group and out-group construction, there are other cultural divisions such as Tehrani (and other big city dwellers) versus provincial dwellers, and Persian versus other ethnic groups entrenched in the society.

What the Green Movement lacks, as reiterated repeatedly by Mousavi recently, is engagement with *all* layers of society and refraining from falling into or perpetuating the divisionist social perspectives. Dabashi also emphasizes the same point and in terms of lower classes asserts that "unless and until these poor Iranians … are actively incorporated into the Iranian political economy, … their legitimate concerns will continue to be systematically abused by a band of illegitimate clerical power mongers."[8]

At the same time, despite the Green Movement's pluralist and transideological stance, the role that the highly ideological, brutal, and violent Islamic Republic is playing in confronting the Movement should be factored in. The (projected) Islamist ideology of the ruling power amounts to a blatant glorification of confrontation and violence. It employs violence as a means to crack down on (in)visible social and political dissent, creating ideological analogies with the history of Islam, hence legitimizing and fuelling more radical and religiously strengthened brutality.

The Green Movement is a struggle to celebrate life and its quality. It has no larger-than-life ideals and as such practically shies away from violence. However, historically, Iranians have not been submissive and have been intolerant of oppression, eschewing subservience, especially when the concerned authority is openly de-legitimized.

13

The *cul de sac* of a demanding, steadfast, irritated, and violence-stricken nation, and the impasse that the custodians of the Islamic Republic are forcefully thrusting on the nation by making no concessions or change whatsoever, may amount to a radicalization of the Green Movement in various ways. Such radicalization could then be pertinent in building the movement's violent antagonistic strength on some particular ideological dichotomization, hence the cycle.

The unbridled violence—perpetuated by the custodians of the Islamic Republic in various forms—cannot solve the Islamic Republic problems with its lack of legitimacy and dealings with the Iranian nation but it may cloud the Iranian post-Islamic Republic sky with confusion and potential exclusionary practices.

Hamid Dabashi

Hamid Dabashi, the Hagop Kevorkian professor of Iranian Studies and Comparative Literature at Colombia University, the author of numerous influential books and articles, a steadfast activist and meticulous observer of Iranian affairs[9] is one of Iran's well-known intellectuals and scholars whose analyses of the developments and changes in the sociopolitical arena of Iran is nurtured by both an intellectually well informed and organically accurate understanding of the collective experiences of postrevolutionary Iran as well as a postcolonial reading of the political history of contemporary Iran which rejects the ideological downplay of one authoritarian period for another. As such, the malfunctioning tyrannical reign of the current Islamic Republic in Iran is criticized without any unreal mitigation on the dictatorial and brutal reign of the pre-revolutionary Pahlavi and its overtly practiced and publicly perceived subservient nature to colonialist powers .

Hamid Dabashi's accuracy in accounting for recent events in Iran, despite being away for decades, is also aided by his admirable efforts and a keen desire to remain connected to ground realities in Iran by monitoring symbolic representations of Iranian society through arts, music, cinema, blogs, books, along with a general endogenous bottom-up approach in scholarly investigation. This affinity with Iranian affairs is also boosted by his endorsing the anticolonial and/or imperialistic and nationalistic—as well as Islamic—aspirations of the Iranian Revolution in 1979 which, in turn, provides a continuity in the historical political struggles of Iranians since 200 years. His interests in Iranian arts, cinema, blogs, and music as sources of insights into the Iranian community have brought about a hands-on flavor to his accounts which is generally and sometimes categorically absent in the political views of Iranian pundits in the United States and the West. As a critical scholar, he has been in a position to notice sociopolitical shifts and changes in Iranian social aspirations which have paved the way for the present popular Green Movement. As such, he has acquired a language that is relevant to all the important sections of society inside Iran as the addressee as well as the outside world that turn into him to understand the Iranian development.

Dabashi's open attacks on the Shah's bandwagon monarchy, American imperialist policies, Israeli atrocities against Palestinians, as well as the Islamophobia in the West, however, have neither swung his views toward making sweeping generalizations and characterization of world into two polemic extremes nor has it forced him into an ethically troubling but politically reasonable realpolitik, that is, to side with the enemy of the enemy. Dabashi sees the Iranian 1979 revolution as a revolt against the unaccountable, tyrannical American protectorate of Shah's regime, which secured the independence of Iran and had a cosmopolitan, pluralist nature but it categorically failed in fulfilling its democratic aspirations and reproduced similar—or perhaps harsher—authoritarian rule after a period of fierce Islamization of the Iranian polity.

Dabashi sees the Green Movement as an extension of the same grassroot struggle of Iranians in attaining democracy, civil rights, freedom, and accountability of the government which can be traced back to 200 years. He has correctly noticed that the Green Movement is inherently a manifestation of the celebration of life in contrast to repeated larger-than-life ideals of the Islamic Republic for the past 30 years, and that the cosmopolitan and pluralistic nature of the Iranian society does not prefer to engage in another classic revolution and violence span, while it has a visionary steadfastness in standing firm on its democratic demands.

Simply put, Hamid Dabashi's work (and approach) is the realization of a famous and yet simple quote of Ali Shari'ati—one of the most influential contemporary public intellectuals of Iran—that "our future should be the continuation of our past." That an all-inclusive, progressive, viable future for Iran *cannot* be envisaged in any form but the one in which a realistic and nonreductionist understanding of the contemporary developments in Iran both before and after the revolution is incorporated. In Dabashi's vision, the right narrative is the one which is inclusive of Iran's 200 years of struggle for democracy and independence and acknowledges the social characteristics of the society as they are.

Dabashi's approach in sociopolitical criticism of the Islamic Republic is a *principled* opposition in contrast to a *political* one. His outspoken cry against the injustice and inequality in various parts of the world and in different contexts, from the neocolonial/orientalist approaches in mainstream trends in social sciences in the west to his well-known works in empowering voiceless Palestinian populations along with his stand against the oppressive Islamic Republic regime in Iran are all made viable simultaneously only through sticking to principles, rather than political siding.

Academically, Dabashi is a fierce fighter against classic/covert Eurocentric and Orientalist approaches and promotes bottom-up context-based, organic accounts of scholarly investigations. As such, he may even find himself at odds with the Left intellectuals who, he believes, sometimes bring about more misunderstanding with their attempts in thrusting the inherited academic legacies in various contexts uncritically.

Hamid Dabashi's admirable knowledge of the political history of Iran, his theoretically sophisticated and eloquent research on explicating the qualities of the Iranian society before and after the 1979 revolution, his signatory love and dedication for his homeland integrated in a universal set of principles of advocacy, and his well-earned insights on realities and developments of the Iranian society have, on the one hand, made him a strong and relevant voice in the recent Iranian struggles for civil rights, and on the other hand, on a wider range, he can stand as an exemplary of a true *principalism* devoid of *strategism* which is radically emancipated and rushes to align with what is right regardless of political consequences. Such an approach is constantly skeptical of power concentration and rejects permanent allegiances to political embodiments and commits itself to rightful principles.

Dabashi's widespread and influential writings on the recent Green Movement in Iran constitute part of his advocacy for the Iranian cause in general. More importantly, these writings are on the basis of a lifetime of scholarship on, and passion for, Iran, while keeping a critical scholarly gaze on Iran and its dramatic changes. By now, Hamid Dabashi is a powerful voice in this movement, a voice which addresses and promotes the cause of the people inside Iran as well as translates the developments for the interested world outside.

The Structure of the Book

The present volume comprises a collection of some of Dabashi's writings on and about the Iranian June 2009 election, its tumultuous aftermath, and the characteristics and aspirations of the emerging Green Movement. These articles, which have mainly appeared in Al-Ahram and CNN, range from Dabashi's encapsulations of the nature of the events and the way the Green Movement needs to be approached in terms of both its historical background and future political consequences to throwing light on the way the developments could best be explained intellectually.

Perhaps, due to the indispensable nature of such writings, Dabashi may discuss different, yet overall relevant, points in a single piece of writing which, in turn, makes the job of thematic categorization of the content hard at some points. Nevertheless, in this volume, Dabashi's writings have been roughly classified into some general sections concentrating on the main issues they deal with. While the tone, the style, and the internal organization of the articles have generally remained intact, some content has been edited in order to best fit the articles and avoid unnecessary repetitions.

The volume starts with Dabashi's diachronic account of the events since June 12—the election day—in which he recaps the highlights of the build-up period to the consequent mass protests. *Diary of a Defiance: Iran un-interrupted* provides an insightful background of the events on the ground. While celebrating the Iranian society agency, the article dismisses the potential "eurocentric" readings of the affairs. In *Ahmadinejad's Fraudulent Election is now a Social Fact*, Dabashi provides an account of the election and deals with the issues and debates regarding the credibility of the election. The section ends with *Bearing Witness* in which Dabashi provides some background information on the role of elections in Iran, discussing how the international community—Obama in particular—can have a positive effect on the Green Movement by simply bearing witness to the struggles of a people.

The next section deals with articles in which the nature and political consequences of the Green Movement are discussed. In his article entitled *The Domino Effect*, the author points out to the international potential and geopolitical consequences of the Green Movement, especially in the Middle East. *An Epistemic Shift in Iran* explores the political background of the Movement and its historical mark on

Iran as a new phase in its struggle for freedom and independence. Dabashi argues that the signs of a shift away from ideology-centered approaches in political change have been visible in Iranian society in the last 10 years within the sociocultural fabric of Iran to which the Green Movement is related diachronically. *Iranian Vote* attends to the dynamics of the presidential campaigns and the unique features of this election which reflects—against the Orientalist notions—the vibrant and cosmopolitan nature of Iranian society. Similarly in *Who won the Iranian Election—and who lost?* Dabashi glorifies the huge social mobilization for the election and argues that the Iranian "supreme leader" and his circle as well as the expatriate opposition groups were the most important losers in this election. *Looking for Their Martin Luther King Jr.* compares the Iranian Green Movement with the American Civil Rights struggles and traces the characteristics of the Movement to the history of violation of rights. The last article in this section, *Easy being Green* discusses the transideological qualities of the Green Movement and evaluates different possible scenarios ahead of Iran.

The following section focuses on the historical political continuity in Iran and explores some of the historically defined characteristics of the Green Movement. In *28-Mordadism: A postmortem,* Dabashi discusses the Anglo-American coup of 1953—28th of *Mordad* of 1332 in the Persian calendar—and traces its trajectory to subsequent political events in Iran, for example, the 1979 Islamic Revolution, the hostage-taking crisis among others. *Returned of the Repressed* historically positions the Green Movement within the immediate to the far-reaching political struggles of Iranians and accounts for the qualities of the political culture in Iran as the genesis of the Green Movement.

The following section intellectually engages with issues of the (il)legitimacy of the Islamic Republic. *The Islamic Republic is Self-Destructing* and *The Moral Meltdown of the Islamic Republic* characterize the most recent actions of the Iranian regime, including its staging of show trials, perpetuating more intimidation, violence, and torture as symptomatic of a publicly visible moral breakdown of the system. He argues that the way the custodians of the Islamic Republic have reacted in terms of the aftermath of the election fraud is a conspicuous affirmation of its lost legitimacy and castigates the system as being neither "Islamic" nor a "republic." In *The crisis of an Islamic Republic*, the author's accent is on the diverse nature of the Iranian society embodied in the "third-way" aspirations of the Green Movement, despite the authoritarian Islamization of the current regime as well as its arch, expatriate oppositional groups who appear to advocate a forceful Secularism. The last article in this section, *The Iranian Baha'is and the American Muslims*, expands on the illegitimacy crisis of the Islamic Republic in terms of its discriminatory practices regarding its ethnic and religious groups, specifically Baha'is, while criticizing the American and Western policies in terms of their Muslim minorities.

Dabashi's reactions and responses to other scholars and/or observers on the Iranian Green Movement and, specifically, his reactions to what is known as the "Left" intellectuals is the subject matter of the next section. He generally dismisses the accounts of the Iranian turmoil in terms of notions of social class and argues that such approaches are intellectually misinformed and misleading if not counterproductive. *Left is Wrong on Iran* addresses Arab intellectual views such as that of As'ad Abukhali and Azmi Bishara as well as the European Left intellectuals' views and criticizes them as missing the realities and attempting to force their own ideological and half-heartedly achieved understanding of the situation to the actualities on the ground. *Looking in the Middle Class in all the Wrong Places*, in turn, elaborates on some of the potential sources of such misunderstandings, focusing on the contradictory class accounts of the Green Movement and the nature of Ahmadinejad's endeavors. Closely related is the article *Adjusting our Lenses*, in which Dabashi shows how the classifications of highly educated middle class urban versus village illiterate poor layers of the society are inaccurate. He argues that some of these enforced categorizations are, in fact, inherited political dichotomies which would not prove to be automatically true. Responding to Zizak and his accounts of the Green Movement in Iran is the topic of a longer writing entitled *The Discrete Charm of European Intellectuals*, in which Dabashi harshly (yet eloquently) criticizes Zizak for what is seen as his readymade application of preexisting intellectual molds on Iran condescendingly and accentuates Zizak's account as a typical eurocentrism of the left.

The focus of the following section is on US politics and its relations with Iran and its Green Movement, specifically the consequences of potential sanctions on Iran. *30 Years ago and Counting* explores the history of the United States in Iran and the highly publicized hostage-taking crisis. Dabashi critically reviews American policies in the region and the US coup against the first democratically elected government of Mossadeq in Iran in 1953. *Katie Couric's Sarah Palin Moment* analyses Katie Couric's interview with Ahmadinejad of Iran and points to some intellectually significant shortcomings in the American media culture. He argues that Katie Couric's failure to attend to important broader—beyond the United States—issues, for example, the Islamophobia, is the breeding ground for the rise of a figure like Ahamdinejad.

A Tale of Two Cities and *The Flawed Logic of a Congressional Hearing* both attend to the role of the expatriate Iranian opposition in the Green Movement and investigate the American grand political policies and the political and economic consequences of the US sanctions against Iran and the way it may be interpreted by the Iranian society is discussed. *Not Millions, just a Quote from MLK will do* more specifically concentrates on the possible detrimental consequences of sanctions as well as the American government's funding projects such as "Democracy for Iran." Dabashi argues that these funds are much more acutely needed and will be fruitful if spent in inner schools and general public awareness raising projects. The last article in this section, *The White Moderates and the Green Movement*, attends to the possible detrimental effects of the so-called moderate American pundits. Dabashi specifically takes to task the reactions of Flint and Hillary Leverett and argues that such half-hearted reactions can have possible detrimental effects on the Green Movement.

The last two short sections have a single article and attend to relations of the Green Movement and the Palestinians and the publicity tactics of the Islamic Republic of Iran in constructing a legitimate face for itself. In *The Arab Roaming in the Streets of Tehran*, Dabashi, in a charming story-telling style, reflects on the struggles of Palestinians and presents a critique on the sporadic Anti-Arab racism seen during the protests in Iran.

The last article in the book, *Staging a Spontaneous Rally*, describes the huge propaganda apparatus of the Islamic Republic which has been at work for the past 30 years and finds similarities in such practices before and after the Revolution. Dabashi argues that the custodians of the Islamic Republic of Iran, suffering deeply from illegitimacy issues, make use of its various bureaucratic, economic, and political leverages to stage a public support show and project a division among the people.

Navid Nikzadfar
June 2010

Notes

1. Dabashi's book, "Iran: A People Interrupted" (2007) provides a rich account of this two-century-old struggle of Iranians and discusses how the contemporary history of Iran is linked to the current struggles in Iran. Abrahamian's book, "Iran Between Two Revolutions" (1982) is now a classic in detailing the political context and development of Iran between the Constitutional Revolution (1911) and the Islamic Revolution (1973).

2. Dabashi provides a highly detailed and enlightening account of the influential Iranian intellectuals who contributed in theorizing such Islamic Revolutionary discourse in his classic book, "Theology of Discontent, the Ideological Foundation of the Islamic Revolution in Iran" (1993/2005).

3. For some details of his speeches before the Revolution and his role as the leader of the Revolution see Abrahamian (1982, pp. 420–479), where he argues that despite his early years of religious conservatism, in the mid-1970s Ayatollah Khomeini followed a political doctrine of avoiding specific Islamic demands and launched his leadership on a general platform of ideals which were in demand since the Constitutional Revolution.

4. Dabashi (2007) argues that the three main political tendencies contributing to the Revolution include "Third World Socialism, anticolonial nationalism, and militant Islamism."

5. "The End of Islamic Ideology," accessible electronically at http://findarticles.com/p/articles/mi_m2267/is_2_67/ai_63787340/

6. "Iran, a people interrupted," p. 346.

7. "The characteristics of Iran's Green Movement," (in Persian).

8. Ibid, p. 229.

9. For a glimpse of Dabashi's groundbreaking academic works on Iran's contemporary history, the origin and characteristics of Islam in Iran, the Iranian new cinema, and postcolonialism, as well as his impressive record of public lectures and activism among other endeavours, see Hamid Dabashi's official Web site at http://hamiddabashi.com/

1

Highlights
of the Events

Diary of a Defiance: Iran Uninterrupted

June 13, 2009

Having just participated in a historic election, millions of Iranians in
Iran and around the world are baffled, angry, and heartbroken with
the official results of the presidential campaign of 22 *Khordad* 1388
(June 12, 2009). There are perfectly legitimate reasons to question the
validity of the official results that have declared Mahmoud Ahmadinejad as the clear winner of this election. The campaign headquarters of
Mir-Hossein Mousavi and Mehdi Karroubi have openly and emphatically questioned the validity of this result and pointed to myriads of
irregularities. The office of Mohsen Reza'i, the other candidate, has
also challenged the results but reserved specific comments for later.
Video clips coming out of Iran show that thousands of Iranian voters
have poured into streets of their capital questioning the validity of this
result, facing brutal suppression of their legitimate and legal protests.
The only thing of which Iranians can be sure and proud is the extraordinary manifestation of their collective will to participate in a massive
democratic process. This unprecedented participation neither lends
legitimacy to the illegitimate apparatus of the Islamic Republic and its
manifestly undemocratic organs nor should it be abused by bankrupt
oppositional forces outside Iran to denounce and denigrate a glorious
page in modern Iranian history. Iranians were right to participate in a
monumental manifestation of their collective democratic will, which
lends legitimacy to nothing other than their political participation, as
it is the indication of nothing other than their democratic maturity.
Whoever the legitimate winner of this election might be, and we may
never get to know that fact, the real winners are the Iranian people—
and no future president of Iran, legitimately or illegitimately occupying

that office, can ever forget or disregard this collective democratic will. This is a cathartic moment in modern Iranian history, which requires collective intelligence, political vigilance, and steadfast diligence to interpret it and move forward. The beleaguered custodians of the Islamic Republic want to see this massive participation as a vindication of their rule. It is not. Bankrupt oppositional forces outside Iran, entirely alien to the democratic aspirations of Iranian people, wish to abuse it to legitimize their degraded positions. They are equally wrong. We need to keep our eyes on the precious ball of a democratic process that has been achieved and handed to us at great cost by generations through their sacrifices. Take a picture of that inky finger with which you voted on June 12 and keep it for posterity. You did the right thing at the right moment, and your children will frame that picture for generations to come.

June 15, 2009

With the semi-spontaneous demonstrations in Tehran and other major cities (including Shiraz, where we have had eyewitness accounts by members of my family), the civil unrest that began on June 13 with opposition to the declared results of the presidential election of June 12 has entered a new phase. The assumption of the election having been rigged is now a "social fact." It is no longer relevant whether or not the election was rigged. Millions of Iranians believe it was, and they are putting their lives on the line to announce and assert it—with at least 12 fatalities, as just reported by *The Guardian*.

We need to have a careful and accurate summation of what has happened so far. On June 12, upward of 80% of eligible voters, about 40 out of 46 million, have voted. This has been the most magnificent manifestation of the political maturity of Iran as a nation and their collective democratic will. This nation does not need, nor has it ever needed, either a medieval concoction called the *Vali Faqih* in Qom or Tehran to patronize it or a Neocon chicanery called "Iran Democracy Project" in Hoover Institution in California to promote it. This nation, as always, can take care of itself. It needs nothing but the active solidarity of ordinary people around the globe to be a witness to their struggles and demand from their media an accurate and comprehensive representation of their movement. So please, hands off Iran! No "democracy project," no sanction, no threat, no military attack, no regime change.

The day after the results were announced, on June 13, there was a spontaneous demonstration in Tehran by supporters of Mir-Hossein

Mousavi demanding recount with an accusation of vote rigging. The following day, on June 14, the government staged a major pro-Ahmadinejad rally in which his supporters were bussed in from surrounding villages. It is important to keep in mind that Ahmadinejad's supporters come from the poorest and most disenfranchised segments of Iranian society, subject to his and his campaign's populism and demagoguery. Based on this fact, one should not conclude that all the impoverished segments of Iranian society, suffering from double digit inflation and endemic unemployment, are on his side or fooled by his charlatanism. The supporters of Mir-Hossein Mousavi and the Reformist movement come from a vast trajectory of Iranian society.

Today, on June 15, 2009, the uprising has assumed an entirely different dimension and may have already transmuted into a full-fledged civil disobedience movement, with hundreds of thousands (according to British Broadcasting Corporation (BBC), which is usually quite conservative in its estimations), demonstrating peacefully and joyously between Meydan-e Enqelab and Meydan-e Azadi. Mir-Hossein Mousavi and Mohammad Khatami have led the demonstration and made speeches, as has Zahra Rahnavard, now an inspiration and role model for millions of Iranian woman. Please take a good look at her and keep her picture and the picture of other women participating in these demonstrations in your files before some other charlatan comes and crops it for the cover of the next edition of *Reading Lolita in Tehran* or else puts together a collage of it for yet another book on "Sexual Revolution" or "Sexual Politics" in Iran. Lipstick Jihadis, career opportunist memoirists, obscene and fraudulent anthropologists on a summer "field work" in Iran, and comprador intellectuals in general are among the main losers of the presidential election of 2009.

What we are witnessing today may indeed be the commencement of a full-fledged civil disobedience, led by an aging revolutionary, Mir-Hossein Mousavi, battle-tested, literally, during the Iran–Iraq War (1980–1988), a war hero to his followers, who then went into seclusion for almost 20 years (reading, writing, teaching, and painting), and has now come back with a vengeance against the opportunistic populism of Ahmadinejad. The movement that he has led has been fortunately peaceful so far, except for at least 12 reported fatalities, perhaps more. Demonstrators have been savagely beaten up both in streets and in student dormitories. But by and large this civil disobedience has been relatively peaceful.

Tomorrow we need to see how the dialectic among three forces will unfold: (1) a mass cross section of society supporting Mir-Hossein Mousavi and demanding at the very least a recount of the rigged votes; (2) the leadership of this movement by Mousavi, Karroubi, and Khatami, and the Reformists in general; and (3) opposing them are the brutal and vicious charlatanism of Ahmadinejad, the autumn of the *Vali Faqih*'s patriarchy initially supporting him, and the platoon of conservative clergy like Ayatollah Mesbah Yazdi in Qom.

Mir-Hossein Mousavi has the makeup of an Iranian Nelson Mandela or Martin Luther King (MLK) Jr. in him. We have to wait and see.

June 16, 2009

It seems to me that the only way that this amorphous movement that is now unfolding in Iran can have a snowball chance in hell to succeed is to become a systematic and comprehensive nonviolent collective act of civil disobedience. To become a more determined and directed social action, this movement will have to assume multiple dimensions beyond a succession of demonstrations in the streets; it must accompany a simultaneous act of discrediting the counter-demonstrations that the regime organizes.

The Majlis (the Iranian parliament) might emerge as one crucial site of contestation—though it is too early to tell. Today in the Majlis, the courageous Qazvin Deputy, Qodratollah Alikhani denounced the way the presidential election has been conducted. This was by no means the sentiment of the Majlis in general, for as Alikhani spoke, Ahmadinejad's supporters were interrupting him, and some 220 of them had in fact written a public letter and congratulated him on his victory. But nevertheless some 52 deputies have summoned the Interior Minister, Mr. Mahsouli, to come to the Majlis and explain what happened yesterday during the demonstration and why demonstrators were shot at, injured, and even killed. These 52 deputies have also been joined by the Speaker of the House, Mr. Larijani, who today condemned the attacks on the student dormitories as well as another attack on Sobhan apartment complex at 2:30 a.m. on 14th June—presumably because defiant chants of *Allahu Akbar* was coming from there. This may all be parliamentary maneuverings to no particular public avail, but something more might be brewing there. It remains to be seen.

Perhaps more important than the Majlis in the snowballing of civil unrest is the demonstration of a group of doctors and nurses at Rasul

Akram Hospital in Tehran. I saw an eyewitness video captured by a mobile phone and dispatched globally. What we see here is the medical staff of this hospital, while still in uniform, coming out of the hospital, forming an impromptu rally, chanting *Allahu Akbar* and then talking to people on the street about the casualties they had treated last night. One of them, a woman physician or nurse, came forward with a sign in her hand on which had been written in Persian (obviously not for foreign correspondents but for immediate public benefit) that the emergency ward of Rasul Akram Hospital had treated 28 people with gunshot wounds, of which 8 have been martyred, asking "Tonight and tomorrow night?" meaning how many more will be murdered? Ordinary people soon gathered around and began applauding the medical staff. Then a male nurse or physician came forward and said to the public that this is only the statistics in this particular hospital, meaning there must be more in others. My point here is not to play the number game about casualties but to point to the planned or spontaneous act of the staff of this hospital to walk out and engage with the public.

If such quiet and dignified civil unrest were to continue to unfold, things might assume different proportions. The BBC reported today that the chancellor of Shiraz University had resigned and that the president of Tehran University has also expressed his concerns publicly. Meanwhile the prominent Iranian vocalist Mohammad Reza Shajarian had issued a statement and asked the national television NOT to broadcast his patriotic songs. They were composed and sung in entirely different circumstances, he said in his open letter, inappropriate for what is now happening in Iran.

This is in obvious defiance of national television that is universally perceived as the main propaganda machinery of the regime and its chosen president. Shajarian is an exceedingly popular and deeply loved public figure, and his admonition of national television carries weight. In the same vein, I saw pictures of famous Iranian footballers sporting green on their wrist bands, and wearing green jerseys as well.

These are the signs we should be looking for in days and weeks ahead. The open expression of solidarity with the movement in multiple public domains will put it outside official control. They are rounding up the usual suspects of the reformist movement. But the movement must now become more universal. The arrest and at times immediate release of prominent reformists like Abtahi, now an advisor to Karroubi, and Said Hajjarian, a prominent theorist and tactician of the reformist movement and the target of an assassination attempt in March 2000, testify to a certain degree of panic on the part of the regime or the commencement of a systematic crackdown. In either case, it is the initially amorphous disposition of the movement beyond the reformist figures that will have a widespread effect.

Counterdemonstrations on behalf of Ahmadinejad are of course well on the agenda. Today Sepah-e Mohammad Rasul Allah (The Army of Muhammad the Messenger of God) called for a pro-Ahmadinejad rally at 4 p.m. Tehran time at Vali Asr Square in order to respond to yesterday's anti-Ahmadinejad demonstration. Anti-Ahmadinejad demonstrators also had a rally that moved toward the Jam-e Jam where the Iranian national television headquarters is located. Mousavi issued a statement to this rally, asking them to be vigilant, law abiding, and peaceful, holding the officials responsible for their well-being and reiterating his request for a nationwide peaceful demonstration. The green color and *Allahu Akbar* remain the sign and the principal slogan of the movement.

The international pressure of course remains quite crucial. I called Paris to talk to Mohsen Makhmalbaf, who is now actively campaigning on behalf of Mousavi's, but learned from his wife Marziyeh Meshkini that he has gone to Brussels (along with Marjane Satrapi) to speak to the European Parliament asking them not to recognize Ahmadinejad's election. Later, I also watched a video of Makhmalbaf giving a speech at a rally in Paris urging Iranians abroad to contact the governments of their respective countries and urging them not to recognize the validity of this election. Ahmadinejad is currently in Russia attending a meeting as the Iranian president. I also saw a circulated e-mail asking for a demonstration in front of Russian embassies condemning their reception of Ahmadinejad as president. According to the *Financial Times*, Russia and China have recognized the validity of the election, while France has expressed strong reservation, and the United States is treading a very thin line. Afghanistan, Turkey, Syria, and Venezuela, according to official outlets in Iran, have congratulated Ahmadinejad. Here is the crucial task of Iranians in places like Australia, India, Japan, the United States, European capitals, Canada, and above all Arab and Muslim countries to pressure their governments if possible or alert public opinion, at the very least, that this election was rigged from the word go, from its very commencement, from the moment that the Guardian Council gets to decide who can run for election and who cannot. The rest is now an academic exercise in futility.

As the movement thus unfolds so does our reading of it become clearer. Richard Seymour has rightly taken issue with me regarding my statement about Mousavi having the makeup of a Nelson Mandela or MLK. I am happy he did, for it gives me an opportunity to explain what I mean. I believe, as I have now said on many occasions, that the only chance that this movement has is as a nonviolent collective act of civil disobedience. I am well aware of the skeletons in Mousavi's past (do please cast a cursory glance at what I teach and what I have written for now almost half a century—yes I wrote my first letter of protest to the governor of Khuzestan when I was eight; though, yes, my mother dictated it to me) and I have referred to them in the Cable News Network (CNN) piece, as I in fact also mentioned it briefly yesterday on GRITtv with Laura Flanders and David Barsamian. I also mentioned that the last major student uprising was in fact during the presidency of Khatami in 1999, 2 years after his landslide victory. Though I voted for Mousavi as the best possible candidate available to us and in solidarity with the nascent movement inside Iran, holding my nose the same way I held it when I voted for Obama. I am no reformer, nor do I shoot from the hip, as it were, when it comes to my careful reading of what is unfolding before us. When I see hundreds of thousands of innocent people peacefully marching in the streets against the might of a brutal and bruised Islamic Republic, I fear the worse. In my opinion, it is too early to tell how the interplay between Mousavi et al. and the volcano they have unleashed will work out. Again, Mousavi is not all that this movement wants, nor is Mousavi totally in control of the movement. There is a dialectic between the two, facing the thuggish brutalities of the regime as they go along. To me, the only way that this movement can come to a meaningful fruition (not just in securing a recount or even a reelection but in fact addressing the wider range of civil liberties) is if it aspires to a nonviolent collective act of civil disobedience that from Gandhi to MLK has always needed a visionary leadership. I am not sure if Mousavi or Khatami are those figures. But I do believe that Mousavi in particular has the public demeanor and disposition of becoming one, the "makeup" of such a leadership—as has in fact Akbar Ganji if he were in Iran now. Someone of that caliber might be able to rise to the occasion. So for the record, my solidarity is with nothing and nobody other than those exemplary and courageous young and old men and women in the streets, with the movement itself, as it unfolds—and in whatever way it opts to define itself and its immediate and distant goals.

29

Beyond this clarification, there is one other crucial issue that I must emphasize here. A key and critical question at this point is the emergence of a new language of revolt that will correspond to the realities of this movement and not be reduced to cliché-ridden, tired, and old assumptions. Any act of theorization of this movement, what exactly is it, and to what extend it will go, must be done exceedingly cautiously and gradually, and in correspondence with the manner in which it is unfolding. But of one thing we can be sure. We cannot allow this movement to be assimilated backward into the existing delusional discourses—whether from the so-called opposition forces outside or the dominant discourses inside Iran. Here I will give two examples. The first example is from the "oppositional" forces outside Iran. Yesterday I saw yet another inane e-mail from Reza Pahlavi expressing his royal solidarity with the demonstrators. Obviously, His Royal Idiocy and the sycophantic band of good-for-nothings that have gathered around him seem to be clinically delusional and under the impression that someone on this side of sanity cares about what he and his criminal dynasty think. As an Iranian citizen, Reza Pahlavi is of course entitled to his opinion about anything. But in matters of politics only after he drops any and all ludicrous claims to that bloody throne that he and his criminal father, and even more thuggish grandfather, left behind when they brutalized and swindled that nation and fled Iran.

Mohsen Kadivar and Liberal Religious Intellectualism

The same is true about the dominant Islamist discourse inside Iran, even when, or perhaps particularly when, it is formulated by the progressive clerics. Yesterday I heard Mohsen Kadivar interviewed on BBC Persian. In conversation with an anchorperson, Kadivar gave an extended explication about how the evident irregularities of this election constitute a breach of the public confidence and is thus a violation of justice and as a result it is incumbent upon juridical authorities to opine on the matter. Now, I know, have met, read, and have a deep affection and even admiration for Mohsen Kadivar, when on numerous occasions he has spoken truth to that brutal power called the Islamic Republic. But there is a crucial issue of which he seems to be entirely oblivious and the time to clear and settle it is right now. This movement cannot be branded in any terms within Iranian political culture, and for one thing it cannot be, yet again, categorically Islamized, juridicalized, or Fiqhified. Let me explain.

Even in the chimerical concoction called "Islamic Republic," we are the citizens of a republic and NOT mere subjects of a medieval jurisprudence, for it makes no difference whether we are the physical subjects of a tyrannical monarch or the metaphoric subjects of a medieval jurisprudence—in both we are denied historical agency and the site of our *public reason*. Unless and until Mohsen Kadivar, as a genuinely progressive jurist, understands this simple fact, we will never ever get anywhere. I for one, again, to repeat, as a citizen of a republic, could not care less what he or any other progressive jurist thinks of my rights as a citizen. That juridical opinion is irrelevant to me, with all due respect. As a Muslim I deny him, and with him the best and the worst of them all together, the authority to transform my agential autonomy as a citizen of a republic into a juridical trope in his (however, progressive or retrograde) jurisprudence. To me, when it comes to this militant or soft, aggressive or gentle, brutal or banal over-juridicalization of Iranian political culture, there is no difference between Mohsen Kadivar and Mesbah Yazdi. They both speak the same juridical language, though from two conservative and liberal ends of it. As a citizen, I no longer wish to be at the mercy of either the criminal backwardness of Mesbah Yazdi or the open-minded liberalism of Mohsen Kadivar. What part of that simple point is incomprehensible? We are in the depth of this misery called the "Islamic Republic" that we are precisely because these people, the best of them, namely Mohsen Kadivar, have made a name and a reputation for themselves and formulated their positions in the absence of any contrapuntal position by people who do not think like they do. Because of them an entire republic has degenerated, and with it a public domain, and with it a *public reason*, into the topography of a variegated jurisprudence from which there is no exit.

Kadivar tells the skeptical anchorperson of BBC Persian that Ulama are infinitely more important in Iran than intellectuals, artists, or even athletes. Now, personally I believe he is entirely self-delusional at this point in history to think that way. But the point of the argument is not between his thinking that he and his ilk are more important to Iranian society by virtue of being a Shi'i jurist than, say, Bahram Beiza'i or Mahmoud Dolatabadi. The point is that within my idea of the republic in which we must ultimately hope to live there is plenty of room for any jurist of any stripe as a citizen. But in the medieval jurisprudence of a Shi'i jurist, however, progressive and open-minded he might be, there is absolutely no niche for me as a citizen—for that jurisprudence, I am already and always transmuted into a juridical subject, a jurisprudential trope, and a mere dialogical trope in his syllogism.

Mohsen Kadivar looks at me and does not see a citizen; he sees a mere subject of his law. In other words, the notion of the *public reason* as the cornerstone of citizenry has not ever crossed the mind of these jurists. I am a Muslim, Mr. Kadivar, as you well know, a Shiite Muslim. I have nothing but love and admiration and utter respect for my parental religion. Since 9/11, I walk and proudly proclaim myself a Muslim in a country and context now Islamophobic to the core. But not all Iranians are Muslims, or Shi'i, or believing or practicing. There are Baha'i Iranians, as there are Jews, Christians, Zoroastrians, and plain old atheists and agonistic Iranians—and God bless them all! But the notion of a republic, Mr. Kadivar, could not care less to what god we may opt to pray or at other times scream out loud upon the dead corpse of a youth just murdered by agents of the "Islamic Republic" and cry our curses. Unless and until you, Mr. Kadivar, the best that our medieval jurisprudence has produced, come to grips with this very simple fact, even this massive movement that is unfolding in front of our eyes will yet again be creatively, kindly, and quite generously Islamized, once again.

We have all been silenced, forced into exile, and by virtue of the absence of freedom of expression in the Islamic Republic never had a chance openly, politely, and respectfully to disagree with this violent or gentle over-juridicalization of our political culture. So Mr. Kadivar, there are perfectly sane (*Aqil*) and mature (*Baliq*) Iranians who, with all due respect, do not give a hoot what the most progressive, open-minded, generous-hearted, Shi'i jurists think of the current crisis we face. Over this *public space*, in which we live as citizens, your jurisprudence has no jurisdiction. You are, of course, as an Iranian entitled to whatever position you may take on the matter. But please check your medieval jurisprudence at the door and speak in the plain language of our common citizenry, with the *public reason* with which we need to build our future republic. Thank you!

June 18, 2009

My fear is that the regime is now shutting down the foreign news agencies as well as the Web sites and social networking in order to get ready for a bloody crackdown. The news from Iran is that the English sites of BBC and CNN are filtered. *Sepah Pasdaran* or the Revolutionary

Guards have threatened the bloggers, twitters, and the Internet users in general with execution, if they are caught disseminating news. But the stream of news is unrelenting. The mourning procession that was conducted today was peaceful and fortunately with no violent incident, to the best of our knowledge. Tomorrow, June 19, during the Friday prayer, though, the scene might be different, for the regime is going to flex its populist muscles by bringing busloads of its supporters.

Where do we stand with the election? Ali Akbar Mohtashami, the head of Mousavi's *Komiteh-ye Siyanat-e Ara* or Committee for the Protection of Votes, has reiterated their position that a *Komiteh-ye Haghighat Yab* or Fact-finding Committee is needed to determine the fate of the election. From Khatami's side there is also a call for either a complete recount by an autonomous entity (and not by those who have created this mess, as he puts it), or even a rerun of the election. Ali Akbar Mohtashami has, on other occasions, called for the election to be conducted again. He has also objected to the *Seda va Sima-ye Iran* or Iranian National Television showing the pro-Ahmadinejad rallies his government had staged repeatedly, creating the impression that this is a *fait accompli*. He has also criticized Ahmadinejad calling the anti-Ahmadinejad rally a gathering of *khar-o-khashak* or thorn and thistle. Qodratollah Alikhani, the Deputy from Qazvin in parliament, has responded to that phrase and said that this flood of humanity against this election is not "thorn and thistle." But by far the most beautiful response to Ahmadinejad calling the masses of millions pouring into streets of Tehran and other cities "thorn and thistle" comes from an impromptu slogan that I heard protesters chant in a subway station:

Khar-o-khashak to'i, Doshman-e in Khak to'i

[YOU are the thorn and the thistle; YOU are the Enemy of this land!]

If you do not know Persian grab hold of someone who does and watch the tears that well up in their eyes when reciting the Persian original. Ahmadinejad's office has issued a statement explaining that he did not mean to dismiss the entire demonstrators as "thorn and thistle" but only the troublemakers. *Keyhan's* choice word for the demonstrators is *arazel-o-obash* or thugs and hoodlums.

Meanwhile the Guardian Council or *Showra-ye Negahban* has allowed for the possibility of the election being altogether annulled. Abbas Ali Kadkhodai, the spokesperson for the Guardian Council has said, "the annulment of the election is not unthinkable

33

[*ebtal-e entekhabat dur az zehn nist*]." The 12-member council has received some 646 complaints about irregularities from the oppositional candidates.

Ata Mohajerani, the minister of Culture under Khatami, has called for something quite baffling. He has asked people to gather in Tehran University this Friday, June 19 for prayer with the leader to tell him about their concerns about their votes. Meanwhile *Keyhan* is picking this very Friday prayer at Tehran University Campus, as an occasion to say *Labbayk* beh *Agha* or We Obey Thy Command, Sire, as *Keyhan* puts it. So, obviously the regime is going to bring busloads of people from around the country to fill out the space. But will pro-Mousavi demonstrators be able to attend the same space? It is quite a bold suggestion by Mohajerani, but also dangerous.

Khamenei remains adamant. BBC reports that he has said, "It is difficult to accept defeat." But this is not exactly what he said. According to *Keyhan*, he admonished both the winners and the losers to be humbled by their victory or defeat. So either *Keyhan* is misinterpreting Khamenei's actual words to make him look more magnanimous than he is, or else, the reformist contingent in BBC Persian are misinterpreting the same words to make him appear more notorious than he is.

The news in Tehran is that the head of the Israeli Musad has said that there is nothing particularly wrong with the elections, that these demonstrations will soon die out, and that Israel prefers to deal with Ahmadinejad. Apropos Israel, BBC also reports, "There are some allegations that right-wing Israeli interests are engaged in a Twitter attack with the aim of causing political instability within Iran." Before we come to any categorical conclusion from all this, let me also add that in his column in Haaretz, Gideon Levy also had a piece in which he said, "It makes one green with envy: The scenes from Iran prove that some nations are trying to take their fate into their own hands. Some nations are not floating on the surface in sickly indifference; some are not looking around in endless complacence. And some are not following their leaders with the blindness of a herd. There are moments in the histories of certain nations when the people say enough. No more." After admonishing the Israelis, he adds, "It's true, there is liberty in Israel, but only for us, the Jews. We have a regime that is no less tyrannical than the ayatollahs' regime: the regime of the officers and the settlers in the territories. But what do we have to do with any of this? In Iran, police disperse demonstrations with violence, they shoot and kill. And what do we do?" You may want to compare this with Seyyed Hassan Nasrallah imbecilic moment, as reported by Noandish, that the "thugs and hoodlums that are demonstrating in streets have no connection to any one of the candidates." This is not to discredit Hezbollah but to mark how decidedly ignorant of this movement the very person of Hasan Nasrallah is, nor should one extend Gideon Levy and a handful of other courageous Israelis to the vast majority of them who have just put Netanyahu and Lieberman in office.

Mousavi, meanwhile, seems to be building momentum around mass rallies and has called for a demonstration mourning the death of people on June 15, to be held on Thursday, June 18. On Wednesday, June 17, Karroubi has called for a black-clad demonstration on Friday, June 29 at 11 a.m. from Tir Square to Friday Prayer gathering. In his letter, he says that he considers the engineered election of Ahmadinejad as *na-mashru'* or illegitimate and that he des not recognize him as a president. He says the June 15 epic demonstration shows (1) people are not accepting this result, and (2) they can demonstrate peacefully.

Tehran University campus, as well as those in Shiraz and perhaps others, continues to be the site of demonstrations. At least one is reported dead and 14 injured—from Tehran University dormitories. Attacks were by both plainclothes and antiriot forces. Demonstrations in Tabriz continue, but it is under a news blackout—all cell phone networks are down—but the news of gunfire shots has reached Tehran. Oroumiyeh is also rising in protest, so is Shiraz, where Dr. Sadeqi, Chancellor of Shiraz University has resigned. Unrest is also reported in Bandar Anzali.

Today, I saw a video, shot and sent via mobile phone, about a subway ride—spontaneous demonstration, without fear—and here are some of their slogans:

Ra' ye ma-ro dozdidan, daran ba-hash poz midan
[They have stolen our vote, and are showing off with it!]
Taqallob yeh darsad do darsad, nah panjah-o se darsad
[Cheating, may be one percent, or two percent, not fifty-three percent!]
Haleh ye nur-o dideh, ray ma-ra dozdideh
[He has seen a halo of light, and then he steals our vote!]
(Referring to Ahmadinejad's claim that he has seen a halo of light surrounding him)

Let me conclude with an e-mail from one of my students who is now smack in the middle of demonstrations in Tehran:

... went to the rally. (don't worry i didn't get into any trouble) i just had to. i was right smack dab in the wave of supporters...i can't even begin to describe what it was like seeing people on rooftops, in trees on cars, on motorbikes, or standing around me, holding V signs and wearing some form of green. mousavi and his humble two cars passed by me and me along with his supporters were gently pushed back into the crowd, like flowers bending in the wind. prof: ja-shoma kheli kheli khalieh. really, truly. to feel the power and might of this nonviolent movement. what an experience i'll never ever forget. all topped off by ferdowsi with a green scarf tied around his neck. in ferdowsi square, someone went to the very top of his monument and adorned him with a green cloth. if you could only have witnessed the cheers and happiness surrounding this one simple, beautiful, powerful act!

Ahmadinejad's Fraudulent Election is Now a Social Fact[1]

In a recent article published both in the *Washington Post* and the *Guardian*, two pollsters, Ken Ballen and Patrick Doherty, have reported that according to their "nationwide public opinion survey of Iranians 3 weeks before the vote ... Ahmadinejad [was] leading by a more than 2 to 1 margin – greater than his actual apparent margin of victory in Friday's election."

That may or may not have been the case, but the abiding wisdom of Aesop's fable of "The Boy Who Cried Wolf" or its Persian version of "The Lying Shepherd" has now made of any such Monday morning quarterbacking an academic exercise in futility. The assumption that the government has rigged the election has now become a "social fact" that millions of Iranians believe and on the basis of that belief have put their lives on the line, with reported casualties of dozens injured and at least one perhaps up to nine people killed. The chief among the slogans of pro-Mousavi supporters is "With God's help victory is at hand/Death to this deceitful government!" Such a significant and sizeable segment of Iranian society has lost its trust in this regime, in general, and in Mahmoud Ahmadinejad's presidency in particular. What we are witnessing before our eyes is a pent-up anger of some 30 years in the making, from the very inception of the Islamic Revolution. The inner contradictions of an "Islamic Republic" seem finally to have caught up with it.

What is unraveling in Iran is not a mere reaction to the result of a presidential election—the tabulation of which may or may not have been accurate. We must place this massive outpouring of pro-Mousavi, anti-Ahmadinejad sentiments from among a sizable segment of Iranian population in a larger context. At least since the presidential election of 1997, which resulted in the presidency of Mohammad Khatami, but with its roots in even deeper sentiments, a vast cross section of society has continuously demonstrated its dissatisfaction with the Islamic Republic. Soon after the election of President Khatami, in the summer of 1999, a major student uprising led yet another massive movement, at a time in fact that an exceedingly popular reformist president was leading the country. Immediately after the tragic events of 9/11 in the United States, a sizable cross section of Iranian youth were rare among Muslim countries that organized a candlelight vigil commemorating the victims of 9/11 in evident and obvious defiance of their government. Even beyond these sporadic or symbolic events, we have a far more sustained record of inborn and grassroots movements in Iran for human rights, civil rights, and above all women's rights, which in many instances have challenged the very tenets of the Islamic Republic.

It would of course be a misrepresentation of Iranian society to presume that the regime in general or Ahmadinejad's government in particular lacks any degree of popular support or legitimacy. Iran is a deeply fractured society, along class, social, and gender lines. The day after the initial demonstrations against Ahmadinejad, his supporters staged a major rally on his behalf. To be sure, these are state-sponsored, well-orchestrated, and carefully staged events, widely broadcast on the national television to fabricate the impression of a far more massive support than he actually enjoys. But nevertheless they do represent a significant segment of the society as well.

What we are witnessing since the June 12 presidential might well emerge as a major civil disobedience movement not just *against* Ahmadinejad but in fact *for* more civil liberties, economic opportunities, human, civil, and women's rights—so far all within the constitutional boundaries of the Islamic Republic—but this may in fact extend to target the nondemocratic institutions within the Islamic Republic, such as the office of the supreme leader and that of the Guardian Council. The militant supporters of the regime are of course wary of the movement and think it as a "velvet revolution" and have warned that they will nip it in the bud. There is already an evident discrepancy between the deep-rooted demands of the movement that this election has unleashed and what Mousavi or the entire reformist movement can actually deliver.

37

In the days and weeks ahead, we will have to wait and see how the dialectic between Mousavi and the volcano he has unleashed will work itself out—but it is false to think that he is all that this movement wants, or that he is in complete control of the movement, or that the ruling clergy will just pack and leave like the Shah did. Mousavi himself has quite a number of nasty skeletons in his closet, from his years as prime minister during the Iran–Iraq War (1980–1988), with his brutal suppression of dissident movements, ideological purging of the universities, etc. He and his wife Zahra Rahnavard are indeed emerging as widely popular in a significant constituency. But that does not mean that this social unrest is just all about him—the only thing that is crystal clear. Out of a population of 72 million, and a total of 46 million eligible voters, some 40 million, upward of 80%, have voted in this election, and a significant segment of them are against the draconian doctrine and policies of the Islamic Republic, the economic calamities (double-digit inflation and endemic unemployment) of Ahmadinejad's domestic policies, and his belligerent positions on a range of issues, from the inanities of his denial of the Holocaust to his vacuous and flamboyant positions on a number of regional issues. Neither can the world at large disregard that collective democratic will and have the delusion of a regime change imposed from the outside, nor can it be brushed aside by the future president of the Islamic Republic, whoever he might be, legitimate or illegitimate. As Grand Ayatollah Montazeri has just said, this movement is challenging the very legitimacy of the Islamic Republic. That the elections might or might not have been rigged is now a moot point and totally irrelevant.

Bearing Witness[2]

If someone were to have asked me 6 months ago what would have been the national, regional, or global consequences of the June presidential election in Iran, I would have said nil—and I am supposed to know better.

Before the unfolding events in Iran over the second half of 2009, national politics had become all but irrelevant in that troubled neighborhood. The geopolitics of the region was landlocked, from Pakistan and Afghanistan to Israel/Palestine and from Central Asia to Yemen, into a terrorizing balance of power, a stifling politics of despair, in which the term "peace process" had contracted into a four-letter word that everyone knew by heart but not one dared or cared to utter.

In the Islamic Republic itself, over the last 30 years, there have been more presidential, parliamentary, and city council elections than probably the entire Arab and Muslim world put together. But these elections were not the insignia of a healthy democracy. They were the desperate signs of an Islamic Republic that was seeking to legitimize a deeply troubled theocracy by the simulacrums of democratic institutions. All that public secret was finally blasted into thin air in just one simple edict this past Fall, when the late Grand Ayatollah Montazeri (1922–2009), the revered jurist who has just been posthumously dubbed the moral voice of the Green Movement said that this regime was neither Islamic nor a republic.

Beyond the Iranian borders, national elections are either a sad excuse for a joke (anywhere from Morocco and Tunisia through Libya and Algeria to Egypt and Sudan to Jordan and Syria) or else regionally inconsequential (from Israel to Turkey) but not so in Iran—not since the June of this year, when the Islamic Republic emerged as the ground zero of a civil rights movement that will leave no stone unturned in the moral fabric of modern Middle East.

Six months into the Iranian presidential election, the civil rights movement that it has unleashed in ever-more creative terms is writing a new page in the modern history of the country and its troubled environs. The children of the Islamic Revolution, systematically sought to be brainwashed into militant zombies by one obscene cultural revolution after another, are turning against their parental banalities like there is no tomorrow. Turning the rhetoric of the Islamic Republic on its own head, this generation of Iranians is using every single occasion since the last June election to challenge the mendacity that has been taught to them. The end of the Islamic Republic, that may or may not come tomorrow, is not the end of the Green Movement, nor are the unfolding ends of the Green Movement confined within the limited imagination of the Islamic Republic or its expatriate nemesis.

This is a cosmopolitan uprising, variedly centered in major Iranian cities, gathering storm in the capital of Tehran, before spilling with a form and ferocity unimaginable in history into a cyberspace rebellion whose full proportions we are yet to fathom. In a New York cab, on my way to CNN studio for an interview, I receive an e-mail from the streets of Tehran and read it on my iPhone, which I use in the analysis I offer 10 min later to a global audience, and my former student in Tehran writes back to say he liked my analysis—"and the cool color of my tie" too!

This is a self-propelling machinery made of Baroque architecture and postmodern engineering, the Haiku-like poetry of Twitters echoing through the arcades and colonnades of the bizarre bazaar of Facebook—all as much banal as beautiful, bordering the supercilious with the sublime!

But how do we recognize, acknowledge, and honor a generation that is smarter, gentler, more forgiving than their parents could ever be—could ever dream?

The Iranian political culture is cleansing itself. The spectacle is no longer solely Islamic. It is Manichean, cosmic, good and evil mixed, and matched to overcome themselves. "Bearing witness" is all, and the most noble, that anyone can do.

Because it has stolen the regional show and drawn it into a dramatic national scene, the Green Movement is very much at the mercy of one major power that can break its back by yielding to Ahmadinejad's preference to distracting the global attention from his domestic troubles. The only man who can paradoxically help Ahmadinejad in his desperate determination to turn everyone's attention away from the Green Movement and toward regional politics is President Obama. One picture of President Obama with Ahmadinejad is a dagger to the heart of the Green Movement that will be remembered longer than the CIA -engineered coup of 1953, which has and will traumatize the US–Iran relations for yet another half of a century.

President Obama's reaction to the most recent phase of the civil rights movement in Iran during the violent crackdown in the holy days of Tasu'a and Ashura has been measured. While he has condemned "the iron fist of brutality," he continues to insist, and rightly so, that "what's taking place in Iran is not about the United States or any other country. It's about the Iranian people," while at the same time insisting that "we will continue to bear witness to the extraordinary events that are taking place" in Iran. That "bearing witness" means and matters more than the president's critics can dream of in their philosophy.

The pressures on President Obama "to do more for Iran," especially when it sports a "Bomb Bomb Iran!" genealogy, must have a term beyond hypocrisy. The Iranian people have every right to peaceful nuclear technology within Non-Proliferation Treaty (NPT) regulations, and the international community has every right to doubt the trustworthiness of Ahmadinejad's government. The worst thing that President Obama can do now, not just against the best interest of Iranians as a nation but also against his own stated ideal of a regional and global nuclear disarmament. is to sit down and negotiate with Ahmadinejad. It will, ipso facto, legitimize an illegitimate government and will never produce a binding or trustworthy agreement with this Iranian president. The alternative to suspending direct diplomacy with Ahmadinejad is neither more severe economic sanctions nor horribile dictu military strike, which will backfire and hurt the wrong people.

The only alternative for the President is to believe in what he has said—"bearing witness," but carry that presidential rhetorical advice to its logical civil society conclusions: Americans should send delegations of civil rights icons, film and sports personalities, Muslim leaders, human rights organizations, women's rights activists, labor union representatives, student assemblies, etc., to Iran. Let them connect with their counterparts in Iran, expose the banality of the illegitimate government that has suffocated the democratic aspirations of a nation for too long.

Over the last 6 months, if the international media has watched or turned away, the Green Movement has been gaining grounds consistently and apace. The regime is giving it all it has, and it does not subside—kidnapping people off the street, murder, torture, rape, kangaroo courts, obscene official Web sites and news agencies making a fool out of themselves by failing to report the truth, distorting it, ridiculing, or else attributing it to phantom foreigners—they have all failed. The Islamic Republic is cornered; the public space is appropriated. Iranians in and out of their country, young and old, men and women, rich and poor, pious or otherwise, are all coming together. "Bearing witness" is an investment in the future of democracy in a country that is destined to change the moral map of a troubled but consistently vital part of a very fragile planet.

Notes

1. An earlier version of this essay was published as "Rigged or not, vote fractures Iran" in CNN.com (June 30, 2009).
2. An earlier version of this essay was published as "Obama's 'bearing witness' is crucial in Iran" in CNN.com (December 30, 2009).

2

The Nature and Political Consequences of the Green Movement

The Domino Effect[1]

Whatever the end result of the current electoral crisis in Iran, the dramatic rise of national politics has already cast a long and enduring shadow over the geopolitics of the region. No country can go "back to business as usual." The climate has changed—for good.

Prior to the June 2009 presidential election, the realpolitik of the region had placed Iran, Syria, the Palestinian Hamas, the Lebanese Hezbollah, and the Iraqi Mehdi's Army on one side of the geopolitical divide, and the United States and its regional allies on another. With an extended foot in Venezuela, Iran had even a claim on the backyard of the United States. In this precarious condition, the Islamic Republic had emerged, not out of its own capacities, but by virtue of serious follies that President Bush had committed in its neighborhood, as a regional "superpower." The presidential election of June 2009 has suddenly made that geopolitics something of an archaeological relic.

With the commencement of the civil rights movement in Iran in June 2009, the moral map of the Middle East is being changed right in front of our eyes, with the democratic will of one nation; in their massive millions and whoever they voted for, having thrown a monkey wrench into the geopolitics of the region. The moving pictures of Iranians flooding colorfully into their city landscape have forever altered the visual vocabulary of the global perception of "the Middle East." Tehran, I believe, is now the ground zero of a civil rights movement that will leave no Muslim or Arab country, or even Israel, untouched. "The unrest in Iran," said the prominent Israeli columnist Gideon Levy of *Haaretz*, recently, "makes me green with envy."

However things may change in the near future. Ahmadinejad comes back to the global scene with a lame duck presidency that may last anywhere from few months, if the mounting opposition succeeds in its demand for a reelection, to a full term if it fails. In either case, there is a domino effect of Ahmadinejad's weakened second-term presidency in the region. The Syrian position in its immediate regional context, from Lebanon through Israel to Palestine, is now seriously compromised. The rushed and injudicious siding of Hasan Nasrallah with Ahmadinejad has joined the fate of the Lebanese Hezbollah with that of the discredited Iranian president. The Palestinian Hamas would now be infinitely more inclined to strike a deal with Fatah and join President Obama's renewed peace process, as the Iraqi Mehdi's Army now has to fend for itself in more pronounced Iraqi (even nationalist) terms and make it easier for the US military to leave.

The domino effect, however, is not limited to the allies of the Islamic Republic and extends well into the domains of its nemesis, for now the options available to both the United States and its regional allies regarding the Iranian nuclear project have also become categorically compromised. The feasibility of economic sanctions or blockade, or a military strike, in the future unfolding of the nuclear stalemate has become increasingly difficult to sell to the international community at large. The heroic fate of millions of young Iranian men and women has now become a global concern. How can you starve Neda Aqa Soltan's soul-mates, or even worse, bomb them?

The democratic will of Iranians has changed the moral map of the Middle East, and the civil rights movement that they have started will have a domino effect that will leave no nation in the region stand where it is. We have to start thinking of a new term for "the Middle East." It is central but to no one's East or West. The Green Movement has recentered the world.

As President Obama wisely keeps Ahmadinejad at arm's length, and as his task in securing a just and lasting peace between Palestinians and Israelis have just been made much easier for him, let it be known that this is the gift that millions of young and old Iranian men and women have just handed him for being a wise and judicious witness to their noble struggle.

A severe crackdown has now dampened the spirit of the civil rights movement in Iran; scores of peaceful demonstrators are killed or injured; hundreds of civic leaders and public intellectuals have been arrested; the leaders of the Green Movement are being accused of treason and threatened with execution; human rights organizations are deeply troubled; and even worse news might still be in the offing. But the morning has broken, and there is much that a simple march of the youth in the United States and around the globe, particularly across the Arab and the Muslim world, all brandishing a green bandana, can do for their momentarily silenced brothers and sisters in Iran. They have sung their native song. They are awaiting the global chorus.

An Epistemic Shift in Iran[2]

For Shirin Neshat and Shoja Azari
In friendship and solidarity
And for having held our hopes high!

About a decade ago, soon after the parliamentary election of 2000 in Iran, I wrote an essay, "the End of Islamic Ideology," in which I made a twofold argument: (1) there is an inner paradox in the heart of Shi'ism that makes it legitimate only when it is in an oppositional posture, and then it loses that legitimacy when it is in power; and (2) the age of ideological convictions was over in Iran, and we had entered a postideological conundrum up for any grabs. I had borrowed the idea from Daniel Bell's 1960 classic, *The End of Ideology: On the Exhaustion of Political Ideas in the Fifties* but radically altered its positivist and functional premise with a dialectical relocation of the argument inside an anticolonial context.

This argument was predicated on my earlier book, *Theology of Discontent* (1993), in which I had demonstrated in extensive detail the formation of a militant Islamist ideology out of a dialectical force that was predicated on a false but enabling opposition between "Islam and the West." My argument in that book was that the false dichotomy was the single most creative catalyst of generating an Islamic ideology and then sustaining its political potency. I argued that "Islamic ideology" was in fact the supreme sign of a fixation with "the West," a delusional mirage that loses its categorical authenticity the closer you get to it.

The radical Islamization of the Iranian Revolution of 1979 had para-doxically turned my own *Theology of Discontent* into an archaeological verification of the exclusive Islamicity of that event, whereas I had in fact written it because that particular militant Islamism was so alien to my generation of activists in the 1960s and 1970s, with a mixture of anticolonial nationalism (Nehru, Musaddiq, and Nasser read through Frantz Fanon and Aimé Césaire) and Third World socialism (Marx read through the Cuban Revolution) as our defining moments. In my *Theology*

45

of Discontent, I wanted to excavate the hidden and distant layers of an Islamism that was in fact quite alien to my generation of leftist activists— not that we were hostile to it but that we thought it (foolishly) outdated. In my subsequent work, I proceeded to place the *Islamic ideology* inside a larger cosmopolitan political culture that obviously included Islamism but was not limited by or to it, a larger historical framework, in which I have always thought Islam is integral but not definitive.

Having concluded that the age of ideology in general and the Islamic ideology in particular was over, throughout the 1990s I took a partial leave of absence from Iranian politics, which I found unbearably boring, and took an extended look at Iranian literary, poetic, visual, and performing arts—film, fiction, poetry, drama, video installations, underground music, photography, etc. It was here that I noted that the creative lexicon of a new generation was in full swing. They were dreaming (to me) unfamiliar dreams. When I wrote my *Masters and Masterpieces of Iranian Cinema* (2007), I opted to write it in an epistolary mode, addressing a younger generation whom I no longer knew intuitively. I had become, unbeknownst to myself, a father-figure to their dreaming otherwise. I was walking on eggshells.

The work of Shirin Neshat was a path of liberation for me—for in her visual reflections, I found a sinuous subway into the subterranean labyrinth of a creative imagination I sensed seminal in what was happening in the postrevolutionary generation. I took the lead from Shirin Neshat and worked my way toward contemporary Iranian, Arab, and Muslim artists around the globe. I followed Iranian cinema very closely, read and watched extensively, and wrote widely on its history, politics, and aesthetics. Around and about Iranian cinema, I began following contemporary Iranian art—its visual, performing, and aesthetic imaginary opening onto a whole tapestry of unfolding panorama in front of me. I was now convinced that the children of the Islamic Revolution had left the political hang-ups of their parental generation behind and were sailing into uncharted territories. They remained conscious and cognizant of poets and artists, and filmmakers and novelists that had animated our souls a generation earlier, but they were making their own mark in newer and more exciting registers. For us Forough Farrokhzad was a poet–prophet who kept us on our toes to reach out to her. For them she was a cute and cuddly grandma who was spoiling her grandchildren—the sheer audacity of these kids, we thought quietly to ourselves, as they were giggling their way around our revered icon and hanging lovely looking pairs of cherry on her wrinkled earlobes.

Shirin Neshat, from *Women of Allah* Collection (1993–1997)

At the writing of this essay, as we are both bruised and enthralled by the presidential election of June 2009 and its aftermath, two almost simultaneous contemporary Iranian art exhibitions, one in New York and the other in London, pretty much sum up the latest that is happening in this domain, where aspects of contemporary Iranian art are on display for the whole world to see—though the operatic panorama of what we are watching in Iranian streets has considerably overshadowed them—for those demonstrations are the variegated vineyard of the wine we are drinking in these exhibitions.

As the colorful drama of postpresidential election 2009 was unfolding in ever-more dramatic vistas in Iran, the global media took very little notice of this astounding presence of young Iranian artists in New York and London. The extraordinarily ambitious "Iran Inside Out," at the Chelsea Art Museum, in New York, curated by Sam Bardaouil and Till Fellrath, was only one among a number of other sites in which some of the most poignant samples of contemporary Iranian art was on display. At Thomas Erben, yet another exhibition, "Looped and Layered," had put together the works of 12 other Iranian artists, as were the works of some 40 other artists, on display in *Selseleh/Zelzeleh*: Movers & Shakers in Contemporary Iranian Art at Leila Taghinia-Milani Heller Gallery. Yet another five Iranians were included among 28 artists in *Tarjama* or Translation at the Queens Museum of Art. Entirely by serendipity, Americans had in these exhibitions all they needed to know about the civil rights movement in Iran right here in these exhibitions, and yet the mass media was chasing "experts" who had scarcely a clue that these pieces of artwork even existed, let alone what they meant.

Shoja Azari's piece in "Iran Inside Out" (Chelsea Art Museum, New York, June 2009).

Bita Fayyazi's piece in "Iran Inside Out" (Chelsea Art Museum, New York, June 2009).

Almost at the same time, in London, "Made in Iran," was a timely, but mostly overshadowed, exhibition, curated by Arianne Levene and Églantine de Ganay, that brought the work of a number of Iranian artists to more global attention.

Shirin Aliabadi's piece in "Made in Iran: Contemporary Art from the Islamic Republic" (Asia House, London, June 2009)

The trouble with the perfunctory media attention that these exhibitions did receive was the habitual false bifurcation the art critics make between *politics* and *art*—disregarding the far more important fact that the traffic between the two sublates the matter into the manner of a whole different way of seeing things. The operatic drama of the Green Movement in Iran was on full display, running the two complementary and/or contradictory urges of patricide and infanticide against each other, and yet journalistic art criticism was still caught in the congested traffic of *art* versus *politics*.

49

From streets of Iran—unfolding of a drama.

It was in the course of my getting closer to the contemporary Iranian visual and performing universe that the presidential election of 1997 and then the student-led uprising of the summer of 1997 came to complement what I was sensing in that universe and convinced me that we are witnessing a seismic change in Iranian youth culture—that a new generation of sensibility was fast upon us. The Presidential election of 1997 and the student-led uprising of 1999 are the two most immediate antecedents of the current uprising in Iran. When Samira Makhmalbaf was invited to Cannes in May 2000 to participate in a conference on "cinema in the twenty-first century," his father and I spent a couple of weeks together in Paris reflecting precisely on this sea change in Samira's generation. A few years later, in 2003, when I went to Cannes to see Samira Makhmalbaf's "Five O'clock in the Afternoon" (2003), I also saw Parviz Shahbazi's *Nafas-e Amigh* or Deep Breath (2003). Shahbazi's film literally frightened me out of my wits and gave me countless sleepless nights. There was a quiet cruelty in that film entirely alien to me, a suicidal serendipity that convinced me that we have entered a whole new matrix of existential anxieties in this generation—at once pregnant with possibilities and yet ruthlessly self-abortive. Shahbazi's film made Albert Camus's *Stranger* or even Dostoyevsky's *Notes from the Underground* read like Tintin comics. The bloody murder of Neda Aqa Soltan will haunt the Iranian Islamic patriarchy for the rest of history. She has finally given a contemporary feminine face to the masculinist martyrological pantheon of Shi'i Islam. A young and exceedingly eloquent Iranian-American,

Melody Moezzi, was interviewed on CNN after Neda Aqa Soltan was murdered, and at one point she said: "When Neda was killed ... she became a martyr ... When we [perform any] physical exertion, Iranians say 'Ya Ali' ... and now we're saying 'Ya Neda.'" There is a whole theology of discontent, a liberation theology of unsurpassed power, in that very twist of Melody Moezzi.

When in 2008, now deeply drawn to the post 9/11 syndrome, once again I turned back to the political parlance of this postideological generation and expanded my 2000 article on "the End of Islamic Ideology" into a book, *Islamic Liberation Theology: Resisting the Empire* (2008). I was ready to make a case for a political culture in which any claim to a liberation *theology* had to move toward a *theodicy*, namely be enabled to account for and assimilate its own shades and shadows, its political nemesis, and emotive alterities—and thus concluded with a chapter on Malcolm X as a figure whose revolutionary authenticity was predicated on cultural inauthenticity—for he kept shifting identity grounds, from a pre-Muslim, to a Muslim, to a post-Muslim, in order to sustain his revolutionary disposition. Sustaining my argument throughout this book was Gianni Vattimo's revolutionary notion of *il pensiero debole* or *weak thought*, and even more than that Emanuel Levinas' palimpsestic constitution of *the face of the other* as the ethical foundation of any future metaphysics.

I had come to this conclusion about "the end of Islamic ideology" and the epistemic exhaustion of ideological Islamism based on the argument that the binary opposition between "Islam and the West" had in fact exhausted its creative energies and thematically dissipated. "The West" had imploded by the end of the Thatcher/Reagan era and the collapse of the Soviet Union and the Eastern Bloc in the late 1980s, which had in turn prompted the publication of Francis Fukuyama's "The End of History" (1989), for now the creative crisis of "the East and West" had depleted itself, and yet within a couple of years, Samuel Huntington published his "Clash of Civilization" (1992) thesis to resurrect an Islamic nemesis for "the West." The events of 9/11 were godsend for Huntington's apocalyptic vision of not just a clash but in fact the end of civilizations. As the world was distracted by the resurrection of an old cliché, I thought we needed to keep our eyes on the ball inside the emotive universe of the younger generation, to whom the internet and social networking had brought down all sorts of factual and fictive walls.

What we are witnessing today in Iran is predicated precisely on that end of ideological thinking, the surfacing of a whole new emotive universe, and the commencement, I believe, of a "civil rights movement" that marks a major epistemic shift in Iranian political culture. This, I propose, is not yet another iteration of a revolutionary uprising, as it is first and foremost evident in the collapse of the binary supposition between "Islam and the West," the exhaustion of both "Islam" and "the West" as potent categorical entities that can generate ideas, sustain convictions, and launch movements in juxtaposition with each other. Bush and Bin Laden, in short, have been protesting too much, and creating a massive smoke screen with their "war on terror" and "jihad," blinding our insight. The ruling clerical establishment and the younger generation they are trying to chain speak two entirely different languages—one a cliché-ridden language of military coup, foreign intervention, and a manufactured "enemy," and the other, the visual, performing, poetic, and dramatic lexicon of a far more fundamental liberation.

In a hasty reaction to what is unfolding in Iran, Slavoj Žižek, a European philosopher, has recently written a useful summary of the most useless and irrelevant readings of the current crisis and then offered his own, in which he suggests that "the green color adopted by the Mousavi supporters, the cries of "Allah akbar!" that resonate from the roofs of Tehran in the evening darkness, clearly indicate that they see their activity as the repetition of the 1979 Khomeini revolution, as the return to its roots, the undoing of the revolution's later corruption … We are dealing with a genuine popular uprising of the deceived partisans of the Khomeini revolution." In other words, Iranians are not going back all the way to the time of the prophet 1400 years ago, but just 30 years ago, and have started their march anew. William Beeman, a prominent anthropologist of Iran, has offered a similar reading. He thinks, "People can only imagine what they can imagine. In Iran, today, both the people and the establishment have only one model for social and governmental change and that is the original Islamic Revolution of 1978–1979. Because both sides are working with the same vocabulary of symbolism, they are groping to command those potent images that will galvanize public support in their favor." Though his vision is foggy because of his ethnographic lenses, Beeman at least offers an archetypal and not a reactionary reading: "The master vocabulary of revolution in Iran is the historical Martyrdom of Imam Hossein, grandson of the Prophet Mohammad, who was killed on the plains of Karbala in present day Iraq in 680."

Both these gentlemen are out to lunch. Not everything that is round is a walnut, as we say in Persian. This is a postideological society, not after reinventing an Islamic Revolution that happened before they were born, or reiterating an archetypal martyrdom that has more than one way to skin a cat. Much has happened in Iran between 1979 and 2009, and neither a revolutionary nostalgia nor an anthropological dyslexia can account for it. Beeman is of course correct that "people can only imagine what they can imagine" (a redundant truism), but he has no blasted clue what this young generation has been imagining, and what their imagining has in turned imagined , far beyond the distorted images of anthropological ethnography. A much more patient reading of the visual and performing arts of this generation is needed before we know what in the world they are doing in their millions, pouring into the streets of their cities, brandishing their poetry and sporting their green bandana. The inherited universe of this generation has been atomized and then radically recast anew. They have reinvented themselves from an emotive ground zero up—not just their parental generation and the aging clergy in the autumn and winter of their patriarchy were fast and deep in the slumber of their siesta when they were out playing and acting out their future. The Iran experts, anthropologists in particular, were also too busy rehashing their old ethnographic notes to notice what these kids were singing and playing. Example? Just take a look at the book that one prominent American anthropologist, Michael M. J. Fischer, has written on Iranian cinema, *Mute Dreams, Blind Owls, and Dispersed Knowledges* (2004), treating the creative bone and blood of a people like the ethnographic evidence of some dead cultural corpse upon which the anthropologist has accidentally chanced and been asked by a coroner to opine.

In the resurrected soul of this generation, no metanarrative of salvation holds supreme, no sublime supposition of truth holds water. They have been after the nuts and bolts of a more meaningful life, from which I have concluded that in specifically political terms what is happening today is far more a civil rights movement than a revolution, a demand for basic civil liberties, predicated on decades of struggle by young Iranian men and women to secure their most basic and inalienable rights. I might well be wrong in my assumption, and there might very well be yet another revolution in the offing, countered by a military coup, opposed by even more severe economic sanctions, even a blockade, perhaps even by a military strike by the United States and/or Israel. No one can tell. But the singular cause of civil rights of

70 million plus human beings, I daresay, will remain definitive to this generation. In the course of these 30 years, this generation has learned from its parental mistakes and might be given the allowance that it is marching forward through a major epistemic shift in Iranian political culture—seeking to achieve their most basic civil liberties within whatever constitutional law that a cruel fate has handed them.

Iranians Vote[3]

"A messianic apocalyptic cult ..."

The Israeli Prime Minister Benjamin Netanyahu's opinion of Iran and Iranians.

By design or by serendipity, the Israeli claim to being "the only democracy in the Middle East" has suddenly been globally exposed for the ludicrous joke that it is.

The June 2009 parliamentary election in Lebanon will go down in history as a major stepping stone for the cause of democracy in that small but vital country. The victory of the March 14 coalition of Saad Hariri, by which they now hold 71 seats in the 128-member parliament, has left the remaining 58 seats to the Hezbollah-led coalition. Israel and its American allies have been quick to paint this election as a victory for "pro-Western" elements and thus a defeat of the Hezbollah. This is not the case. Exactly the opposite is the case. The victory of the March 14th coalition is the victory of democracy in Lebanon—a victory in which Hezbollah was integral, a democracy now definitive to Hezbollah. Because Israel is a racist apartheid state, it cannot see the world except through its own tribalist lenses. The victory of the March 14th coalition in Lebanon is the victory of the electoral process, which now solidly includes Hezbollah and its parliamentary allies. Hezbollah is now part and parcel of the Lebanese civil society, political apparatus, and institutionalized democratic process—and Hezbollah has achieved this without abandoning its status as a national liberation army that will defend its homeland against any and every Israeli barbarity that may come its way. This is not a defeat for Hezbollah. It is an infinitely more solid victory than if its coalition had won 71 and lost 58 seats. But Israelis are too busy being an apartheid state to see this.

As the Arab and Muslim world celebrates this democratic victory, it is imperative to see it as absolutely having nothing to do with Obama's presidency or his speech in Cairo—lecturing Muslims in the region on democracy, while his army is illegally occupying Iraq and slaughtering Afghans.

On the heels of the Lebanese election, the cause and the march of democracy has had an even bolder site to celebrate in neighboring Iran—and that celebration is not because of American promotion of democracy but, in fact, despite and against it. At the writing of these words, millions of Iranians in and out of their homeland are deeply angry and heartbroken with the official results of the presidential campaign of 22 *Khordad* 1388 (June 12, 2009). Some go so far as considering what has happened as a *coup d'état*. There are perfectly legitimate reasons to question the validity of the official results that have declared Mahmoud Ahmadinejad as the clear winner of this election. The only thing of which at this point Iranians can be sure and proud of is the extraordinary manifestation of their collective will to participate in a massive democratic process. This unprecedented participation neither lends legitimacy to the illegitimate apparatus of the Islamic Republic and its manifestly undemocratic organs nor should it be abused by bankrupt oppositional forces outside Iran to denounce and denigrate a glorious page in modern Iranian history—and it is precisely this democratic process that at this point needs critical attention.

Every 4 years during the presidential election, followed by every parliamentary election, in the Islamic Republic of Iran, the central paradox in the making of this democratic theocracy fascinates and baffles the world. During this presidential campaign, Iranians bois- terously joined rallies and then stood in long queues to vote in their 10th presidential election since the Islamic Revolution of 1977–1979 under the extended shadow of Israeli warlords threatening them with a military strike. The propaganda machinery at the disposal of Israel will have the world believe that a populist demagogue like Ahmadinejad is "the dictator" of Iran and thus on the model of an Oriental despot he represents a backward people whose fate deserves to be determined by others—the United States and/or Israel, of course. As the prominent Israeli scholar of Iran, Haggai Ram, one of a handful of courageous Israeli dissidents, has aptly demonstrated in his *Iranophobia* (2009), the Israeli fixation with Iran has now reached entirely pathological proportions and is a case study of self-delusional hysteria that keeps feeding on itself.

The reality of Iranian polity, as the world has now once again been witness to, is vastly different from the picture that the United States and/or Israeli propaganda machinery is feeding the world. A vibrant and restless society is defying all the mandated limitations on its defiant will and demanding and extracting its democratic rights . The undemocratic institutions of the Islamic Republic—beginning with the very idea of *Velayat-e Faqih* down to the unelected body of the Guardian Council—are not obstacles to democracy in Iran but in fact invitations to democratic assault. What the Iranian electorate, young and old, men and women, seems to be doing is far more important than a mere head-on collision with these aging and arcane institutions. They are pushing the limits of their democratic exercises in unfathomable and thus unstoppable directions. The Internet has connected the Iranian youth to the global context, and they have in turn become the catalyst of discursive and institutional changes beyond the control of the clerical clique in Qom and Tehran.

This, more than anything, is a battle between generations. Iranian society is changing and is changing fast. The aging custodians of the Islamic Republic wish to sustain a very limited discourse of what can be said or expected. But the globally geared and wired youth, more than 60% of the electorate, is now radically altering the very contours of that limitation. They are not merely defying it—they are subletting it. There is a red line in political discourse in Iran that is thinning by the hour, for facing it are skilful players exercising their political muscles. It was quite evident in the course of the US presidential election of 2008 that an Internet savvy Obama campaign outmaneuvered McCain's arcane operation. The same is true of Mir-Hossein Mousavi's and Mehdi Karroubi's campaign, the two reformist candidates, on one side, and Ahmadinejad's on the other, with Mohsen Reza'i's in between. The social basis of Mousavi's platform is the urban middle class, the youth, and women. The economic basis of Ahmadinejad's demagoguery is the rural and urban poor. They are both skilful campaigners in reaching out to their respective constituencies.

The rising demographic tide is against the old revolutionaries. Iranian children born after the revolution in the late 1970s have no active memory of its hopes and furies and could not care less about those who do. Every 4 years since the end of the Iran–Iraq War in 1988 and the death of Ayatollah Khomeini in 1989, the Iranian electorate has been upping the ante. They voted for Rafsanjani in 1989 and for 8 years he rebuilt the economic infrastructure of the country after the war, created a class of *nouveau riche*, foregrounding an economically fractured society. Then in 1997 they voted for Mohammad Khatami who gave them a modicum of civil society and opened the vista of wide-ranging social reform and yet did nothing, or very little, to

56

alleviate the poverty of the masses that Rafsanjani had left behind. In 2005, they, meaning those disenfranchised by Rafsanjani's economic projects and indifferent to Khatami's social and cultural agenda pushed both Rafsanjani and the Reformist aside and yielded to the populists power of Ahmadinejad. And now in 2009, a major segment of the disaffected voters, in their massive millions, are investing their trust in Mir-Hossein Mousavi—a former prime minister with impeccable revolutionary credentials, a war hero, and a socialist in his economic projects. This time around, again, the scene is overwhelmed by the massive participation of the youth, the students, and above all women—on both sides of the political divide. This new generation is Internet savvy, versatile with Facebook, Youtube clips, and Twitter. It is globally wired. The presence of Zahra Rahnavard, Mousavi's distinguished wife, is an added momentum in this campaign. A prominent public intellectual and a former university chancellor, a poet, painter and sculptor, and a staunch advocate of women's rights, Rahnavard is dubbed by some foreign journalists in Iran as the Michelle Obama of Iran. "No," has retorted one of her Iranian admirers in response, "Michelle Obama could have aspired to become the Zahra Rahnavard of the United States."

This particular presidential election has also been extraordinary because of live televised debates, which has spilled and exposed all the skeletons collected in some 30 years in the closets of the aging elders of the republic. Ayatollah Khomeini died triumphant, thinking he was God's gift to humanity. His closest allies, Rafsanjani and Khamenei, are alive and well, witnessing the daily corrosion of their revolutionary pasts, as they see an upstart demagogue like Ahmadinejad discredit and dishonor them all. Ahmadinejad is the bastard son of the Islamic Revolution—its populist, fascistic, demagoguery now returning to devour its idealism and aspirations. Opposing Ahmadinejad are the architects of Iranian creative imagination. More than ever, Iranian artists and filmmakers have been active in this election. They have published open letters, produced video clips, and joined their fans in their rallies. From Paris, Mohsen Makhmalbaf wrote an open letter, supporting Mousavi and encouraging everyone to vote for him, while dispatching his youngest daughter Hana to go to Iran to make a documentary about the election. When the official results of the election were challenged by Mousavi, Makhmalbaf became a conduit of his campaign with international news outlets, using his vast connections with foreign journalists. Majid Majidi, another prominent

Iranian filmmaker, directed Mousavi's campaign commercials. Other Iranian directors, actors, and producers have put their efforts together encouraging Iranians to vote (for Mousavi). Student organizations, labor unions, professional associations, and women's rights organizations—everyone has been in the streets, on the Internet sites, writing fiery essays, taking moving pictures, producing clever video clips. Zahra Rahnavard, a painter with a eye for color symbolism chose the color of green for her husband's campaign—neither the red of violence nor the white of martyrdom—the other two colors in the Iranian flag. Suddenly one day a human chain held the Iranian capital in the bosom of its warm embrace, all the way from Tajrish in the north to Meydan Rah Ahan in the south. When Khatami went to Isfahan to campaign for Mousavi, upwards of 100,000 people came together in the historic Meydan-e Naqsh-e Jahan (now called Meydan-e Imam Khomeini) to cheer him and support the reformist candidate. This is no mere theocracy; this is no dictatorship, like Bollinger said on behalf of the US and/or Israeli Zionists. This is a democracy from below, a democracy not by virtue of institutions that deny it, but by virtue of a collective and defiant will that insists upon, demands, and extracts it. Israeli warlords should think twice before dropping any bomb on these people.

Disappointed by this democratic process are not just Israeli and American Zionists as they see these seas of humanity pouring into streets to steer the destiny of their homeland. Having spent much time and money portraying Iran as a diabolic dictatorship deserving to be bombed to behave, they now have to face the banality of their own evil. Equally scandalized by this election are this colorful band of lipstick jihadi, Hirsi Ali wannabes who are writing one erotic fantasy after another about "Iranian women," over-sexualizing Iranian politics as they opt for "love and danger" during their "honeymoon in Tehran." Look at the picture of these young and old Iranian women in the rainbow coalition of their magnificent participation in the democratic destiny of their homeland—marching in the streets, campaigning for their preferred candidates, distributing pamphlets, organizing rallies, publishing moving articles, making creative video clips in support of their cause. Have a full mental picture of these women, or better still prepare an archive of their pictures before yet another Azar Nafisi crops them out of their noble context and have them read *Lolita* in Tehran, or else another Pardis Mahdavi cuts and collages them and have them have sexual orgies in Tehran. The representation of these women in the flea market of the US publishing industry began under President Bush with Azar Nafisi's *Reading Lolita in Tehran* (2003) and has now come to a new depth of depravity in Pardis Mahdavi's *Passionate Uprisings: Iran's Sexual Revolution* (2009)—one reducing them to little Lolitas gathering around a latter-day Scheherazade and now the other having them shoved into a sexual orgy. Between a *haram*-full of Lolitas and a bath full of nymphomaniacs is where Azar Nafisi and her progeny Pardis Mahdavi have Iranian women marching in despair awaiting liberation by the US marines and Israeli bombers. What a band of miscreant banality is this platoon of expatriate Iranian women memoirists and anthropologists—utterly irrelevant in the democratic struggles of their country of origin and even more useless for any noble cause in the country where they live. Advancing their myopic personal careers as they feed the masculinist fantasies of a belligerent empire, they produce banalities that scarce anyone reads except to confirm their forgone conclusions. Look at the streets of Tehran. Do any one of these women look like they have just been reading *Lolita* or waking up from an orgy?

On two sides of Iran lay in waste Iraq and Afghanistan, liberated for democracy George W. Bush and now Barack Obama style. In the middle, millions of Iranians who would have been maimed or murdered by a similar "liberation" peacefully poured into streets and jubilantly marched to polling stations to vote—in a grassroots, inborn, however limited and flawed, but still promising and beautiful, march toward democracy. And now that they think their votes have been stolen from them they are more than capable of demanding it back—in a long, lasting, and undaunted march to victory.

Whoever the final winner of this election might be (and the official, entirely unreliable, indications are that it is Mahmoud Ahmadinejad), fanatical Zionists in Israel and the United States, power-mongering Mullahs in Tehran and Qom, and comprador intellectuals and career opportunists from Washington DC to California are its sorest losers. The winners are the indomitable Iranian people—men, women, young, and old—whoever their candidate of choice might be. This is a triumph of democratic pluralism, from Lebanon to Iran—the nightmare of the Jewish state that wants the whole region and with it the whole world in its own fanatical image: a delusional, racist, apartheid state, where sects and factions fight each other to their dogged end. Take another look at the quotation from the Israeli Prime Minister with which I opened this article: "A messianic apocalyptic cult ..." Indeed a very apt and appropriate description, but certainly not of Iran—instead, of a country and clime much closer to Netanyahu's own heart. In a remarkable act of psychopathological projection, the chief zionist in charge of the only apocalyptic messianism that has gathered a cult of fanatics in the region calls his nemesis what his own colonial settlement is to the rest of the world. Mr. Prime Minister protests too much.

Who Won the Iranian Election—and Who Lost?[4]

Khonak an qomarbazi keh bebakht har cheh budash,
Benamand hichash ella havas e qomar e digar.
[Lucky that gambler who lost all he had,
Left with nothing but the urge for yet another game]

Rumi

The Iranian presidential election of June 2009 will go down in history as one of the most magnificent manifestations of a people's indomitable will to achieve enduring democratic institutions. The beleaguered custodians of the Islamic Republic are so thoroughly aware of their own lack of legitimacy that they are quick to use the occasion as a vindication of their illegitimate rule. They are wrong. This was not a vote *for* their legitimacy. It was a vote *against* it—within the medieval juridical fortress that they have built around the noble notions and principles of citizenry in a free and democratic republic. The feeble "opposition" to the clerics abroad is equally rushed to admonish those who participated in the election, insisting on regime change, at a time when upward of 80% of eligible voters have actively and willingly participated in the election. Both these desperate, hasty, and banal readings of the election, predicated on bankrupt positions are false and conceal a far superior truth.

Let us begin with the losers of this presidential campaign—first, the single most important loser of the Iranian presidential campaign of June 2009 is Ali Khamenei, the supreme leader, and the *Vali-ye Faqih*. If this election, the *process* of the election not its fraudulent result, showed anything it should, this nation is not supremely *Safih* or indigent to need a Supreme *Faqih* or Most Learned to shepherd or chaperon it. This election revealed the political maturity of a nation that perhaps can now be allowed to return to its own devices and the obscenity of the very notion of a *Vali Faqih* wiped off its body politic. The very office of the supreme leader is an insult to the democratic intelligence and the collective will of this nation, an effrontery to its republican will. If Ali Khamenei had an iota of decency left in him, in the autumn of his patriarchy, he would dismantle this obscene office forever, convene a constitutional assembly and disband the other three undemocratic institutions of the republic—the Assembly of Experts of leadership, the Guardian Council of the constitution, and the Expediency Council of the regime. These are the enduring vestiges of a theocratic legacy that have no room in a democratic republic. Iranians are Muslim, the vast majority of them, and there are millions of Iranians who are not Muslim, or believing or practicing Muslims—and none of that should matter in their privileges and duties as citizens of a republic. As he witnesses the erosion of every single iota of legitimacy that the Islamic Revolution claimed over the nation, the soon-to-be 70 Ali Khamenei can leave a legitimate legacy for himself by seeing to it that this medieval banality is wiped out of Iranian democratic aspirations . It is simply unseemly to see grown people, Ahmadinejad or Mousavi, appear so obsequious and sycophantic toward another man. What is the difference between a Shah and a supreme leader? Nothing.

An equally important loser in this campaign, though declared its winner, is the populist buffoon of that unsurpassed charlatan Mahmoud Ahmadinejad, the bastard son of the Islamist revolution. In his demagoguery and fanaticism, he represents and reveals the most fascistic tendencies of the Islamic Revolution and republic from their very inception. All revolutions have a dose or two of populism and demagoguery mixed with their idealism and high aspirations. What has happened to, and in, the Islamic Revolution is that its innate populism has now been personified in one demagogue who seeks to stay in power by manipulating the poor and disenfranchised segments of his constituency by fraudulent economic policies that gives a person a fish instead of teaching them how to fish, gives governmental subsidies and handouts instead of generating jobs—in an oil-based economy that is already incapable of creating jobs. The economic policies of Ahmadinejad have been catastrophic and institutionally damaging, causing double-digit inflation and endemic unemployment in an oil-based economy at the mercy of global market fluctuation far beyond Ahmadinejad's control or even comprehension. His religious populism and ludicrous claims to divine dispensations is a cruel joke on signs and symbols people hold sacred.

The next loser of this election was Mir-Hossein Mousavi's rather poorly run presidential campaign—ill-advised, ill-prepared,

61

sentimental, full of necessary color symbolism but lacking in substance, in a clearly articulated platform, in economic detail, in political programming, in reaching out to a wider spectrum of his constituency. His campaign was too elitist, trapped, in its visual paraphernalia, inside too excessive attention to Northern Tehran's sensibility and lacking substance in the most fundamental issues of an oil-based economy. His delay in entering the race, his "back-and-forth" dealings with Mohammad Khatami was an indication of poor preparation, as was his debate with Ahmadinejad. While Ahmadinejad had come with charts and graphs and dossiers, flaunting his lumpen demeanor, thinking himself as "a man of the people." Mousavi had nothing except his gentility to offer. He rambled along, read from written statements in a barely audible voice, ran out of things to say before even his time was over.

The problem with the Iranian democratic movement is not that it is unable to produce an Obama—if he is the model. Mir-Hossein Mousavi could have very well been an Iranian Obama. The problem is that there were no David Axelrod or David Plouffe, what Mousavi's campaign desperately needed and sorely lacked. A band of self-indulgent postmodern Muslim yuppies seem to be around him with evidently not an iota of awareness on how to reach his multiple constituencies. If Mousavi did reach these constituencies it was because of his credentials as a war hero (to his supporters and comrades-in-arms), for having saved the integrity of the country during the Iran–Iraq War (1980–1988). But he faced a new Iran, a new generation, an entirely different constituency that loved and admired him and his wife Zahra Rahnavard, on their face value. But you never win a campaign on just good will. This is not to suggest that the election was not rigged; that it was rigged is now a social fact, and a moot question. But there are rudimentary strategies of reaching out to diverse constituencies, which his campaign ignored.

The next big loser in this Iranian election was the legacy of George W. Bush, of the Bush (Wolfowitz) doctrine. Look at Iraq, Pakistan, and Afghanistan, on two sides of Iran, and then look at Iran on June 12, 2009. Millions of Iranians in a peaceful, orderly, joyous, and enthusiastic manner marched to their ballot boxes. The second they thought their votes were stolen they poured into the streets—what Americans should have done in 2000. Along with Bush and the Wolfowitz doctrine, the US congress, and its headquarters at The American Israel Public Affairs Committee (AIPAC) were also the losers.

The US congress can scarce be imagined more transparently hypocritical. On the night before the Iranian election on June 12, AIPAC pushed a button and its stooges in the US congress began pushing for a resolution imposing more severe economic sanctions on Iran, knowing only too well that the following day its news would increase the chances of Ahmadinejad—Israel's chosen candidate, as the Israeli officials have been only too eager to admit.

Losers are also expatriate Iranian monarchists along with all other politically bankrupt banalities and their native informers and comprador intellectuals, establishing vacuous centers for "dialogue" or else centers to save "democracy" in Iran. What a band of buffoons they were made to look, after this grassroots and innate desire for democratic rights.

The sole winners of the presidential election 2009 were Iranian people, whoever they voted for—some 40 million of them, out of an eligible voting population of 48 million, upward of 80%. By virtue of this election, it is perfectly evident that the democratic will of Iranians has now matured beyond any point of return, no matter how violently the unelected officials of the Islamic Republic wish to reverse it. It is too late. As evident during the presidential election 2009, Iranians are perfectly capable of organizing themselves around competing views, campaigning for their preferred candidates, peacefully going to polling stations and casting their vote. It is high time that the Shi'i clerics pack their belongings and go back to their seminaries, as it is long overdue for regime change charlatans like Paul Wolfowitz to retire in ignominy, and for career opportunist comprador intellectuals of one think tank or another in Washington DC or Stanford University to go back to their teaching positions they had before.

Before I close, I must also say that a major loser of this presidential election in Iran is Hassan Nasrallah of Lebanon. Mr. Nasrallah must know that the deep and variegated roots of Iranians' commitment to the Palestinian cause and the fate of the Shi'is in Lebanon are in the vast ocean of their hearts and minds, fed to them with their mother's milk and buried in their shroud, and *not* in the dirty pool of Ali Khomeini's pocket . Arabs in general and Palestinians in particular ought to know that Iranians are watching them closely and wish to hear their voices. This is the Iranian Intifada. A leading slogan in the streets of Tehran is *Mardom chera neshestin, Iran shodeh Felestin* or People why are you sitting idly by, Iran has become Palestine. Arab and Muslims, and their leading public intellectuals must come out and take the side of this grassroots, innate, and peaceful demand for a healthy and robust democracy.

The US congressional stooges of AIPAC, as well as the Israeli generals, are all squarely on the side of Ahmadinejad. This puts them in the same league as Hassan Nasrallah. This is not a warning only to Hassan Nasrallah. All Arab and Muslim potentates ought to know that their youth are watching the events in Iran with a keen interest. It is not only the Iranian youth that are wired to Facebook and Twitter, so are their brothers and sisters around the globe, throughout the Arab and Muslim world. Young Arab and Muslims around the globe are not unaware of the demands that young Iranians are exacting at the heavy cost of courageously exposing their bare chests against bullets and batons of tyranny. This is a postideological generation. They could not care less about their parents' political hang-ups. They demand and will exact their human, civil, and women's rights, through a grassroots, innate, and entirely legitimate uprising—without compromising an inch to the imperial operation of the United States or the colonial thuggeries of Israel. This is not a revolution to topple the Islamic Republic, this is a grassroots demand for civil rights. Iranians being clubbed and shot in the streets of Tehran are not the stooges of the United States. The Arab and Muslim medieval potentates suffocating the democratic aspirations of their people are. Fear the day that young Arab and Muslim youth will learn from their Iranian brothers and sisters and demand and exact their inalienable, human, civil, and women's rights, freedom of peaceful assembly, freedom of expression, equal rights for men and women, economic opportunity, respect for human decency, and rule of law.

Looking for Their MLK Jr.[5]

Though the sudden outburst and the spiralling crescendo of the events did indeed jolt me when it occurred, many aspects of the current crisis in Iran are not surprising to me at all. That the ruling apparatus of the Islamic Republic were out of touch with the ideals and aspirations of a new generation of Iranians has been evident at least since the presidential election of 1997 that brought the icon of the reformist movement Mohammad Khatami to power. The student-led uprising of the summer of 1999 further demonstrated that there is a sea change in the demographic underpinning of the Islamic Republic, with upward of 70% of its young population under the age of 30. That upsurge of youthful euphoria hit a plateau and changed gear during the second presidential campaign of Khatami in 2001 when he had obviously failed to deliver on his prior campaign promises.

If you were to follow aspects of the youth culture in Iran at the turn of the century—from the rise of a fascinating underground music (particularly rap) to a globally celebrated cinema, an astonishing panorama of contemporary art, video installations, photography, etc.—you would have noted the oscillation of this new generation between apathy and anger, frustration and hope, disillusion and euphoria. In their minds and souls, as in their Blogs and electronic chat rooms, they were wired to the globalized world, and yet in their growing bodies and narrowing social restrictions trapped inside an Islamic take on the Calvinian Geneva.

To me, this soon appeared as a postideological generation, evidently cured of the most traumatic memories of its parental generation, from the CIA-sponsored coup of 1953 to the Islamic Revolution of 1979. The dominant political parameters of Third World Socialism, anticolonial nationalism, and militant Islamism that divided my generation of Iranians seems to have lost all validity in this generation, and as a result, I see the moment we are witnessing as, if anything at all, a civil rights movement rather than a push to topple the regime. So if Rosa Park was the American "mother of the Civil Rights Movement," the young woman who was just killed point blank in the course of a demonstration; Neda Aqa Soltan, might very well emerge as its Iranian daughter.

If I am correct in this reading, then in my judgment, we should not expect any imminent fall of the regime on the model of either the Shah's or Saddam Hossein's. These young Iranians are not out in the streets seeking to topple this regime, for first, they lack any military wherewithal to do so, and second, they are alien to any militant ideology that may push them in that direction. It seems to me that these brave young men and women have picked up their hand-held cameras and shoot those shaky shots, looking in their streets and alleys for their MLK, as opposed to my generation that still hangs a portrait of Malcolm X in their homes and offices. These young Iranians are well aware of Mir-Hossein Mousavi's flaws, past and present. But as the color of green, which has spontaneously surfaced from the hearts and minds of his supporters, the very figure of Mousavi, it seems to me, is a collective construction of their innermost desire for a peaceful, nonviolent achievement of their human, civil, and women's rights. Like a water lily from the calm surface of a suspicious pool, they are picking Mir-Hossein Mousavi up and holding him as their highest hopes. They are facing an army of firearms and fanaticism, while chanting poetry and waving their green bandanas. I thought we had courage to take up arms against tyranny. Now I tremble with shame in the face of their bravery.

Easy Being Green[6]

A week of mourning for a revered spiritual mentor of a national uprising, 6 months of massive street demonstrations in the aftermath of the presidential election of June 2009, a decade of pent- up anger after the student-led uprising of July 1999, three decades of frustration after the violent consolidation of an Islamic Republic, 100 years of innocent expectations after the writing of a first constitution, and two centuries of dogged determination in the relentless struggle of a people to secure democratic institutions are all hidden and manifest in every shaky camera shot you see streaming down your You Tube links and finding its ways to your Facebook and Twitter accounts, showing them to all the friends you share. It may all look fuzzy and furious—but there is method in it.

The paramount question the world asks itself these days, 6 months into the making of the Green Movement: Will the Islamic Republic fall? Is this yet another revolution in the making, just like the one we saw in 1979, or will the military apparatus of the Islamic Republic come out like a fully charged armadillo and run through the streets of Tehran and other cities and turn Iran into a theocratic dictatorship, ruled by a military junta like Pakistan, clad in an ideological fanaticism it will have borrowed and expanded from Molla Omar and the Afghan Taliban?

For the last 6 months, and since day one of this uprising, lovingly code-named the Green Movement (*Jonbesh-e Sabz*) I have consistently called and continue to call it a *civil rights movement*. This does not mean I am blind to its revolutionary potentials, violent dimensions, or destructive forces. It does not mean that the Islamic Republic may not, or should not, fall. I keep calling it a *civil rights movement*, though it may come to pass that we will actually see an end to the Islamic Republic, because I believe that the underlying social changes that have caused and continue to condition this movement are hidden under the smoke screen of its political smoke screen. As our highfaluting attention is distracted by the politics of the moment, I have kept my ears to the ground listening to the subterranean sounds and tremors of an earth holding some 200 years of an anticolonial modernity in it sinuous silence.

Beyond the pale and patience of politics, and the attention span of a twitter phrase or a Facebook prose, I have also called this a civil rights movement for I see something in that polyclonal green that defies augury. That color green is a sign that signals and means many things to many people, and no one is entirely in charge to legislate or regulate what it is exactly supposed to mean. It is just a color, a sign, and under it, have swarmed disobedient signals that have just broken loose of the Bastille of legislated semantics of a political culture, of its power and authority, form and manners, rules and regulations. Green is now free floating in a multifaceted *Farbenlehre* that respects no judge, jury, or hangman.

For 30 years, not just over the last 6 months, the Islamic Republic has systematically and consistently distorted a cosmopolitan and multifaceted political culture and (by hook or by crook) shoved it down the narrow and suffocating chimney of a militant Islamism that is of course integral to that culture but has never been definitive to it. From anticolonial nationalism to Third World socialism (all with an enduring feminist underpinning) they have been equally, if not more, definitive to that political culture. The Islamic Republic, as we know it today, is not a state apparatus—it is, as it has always been, the penultimate result of successive scenarios of crisis mis/management: from the American Hostage crisis of 1979–1980 to the Iran–Iraq of 1980–1988, from the mass executions of dissidents in 1988 to the Salman Rushdie Affair of 1989, and from then on the successive Gulf Wars, the Israeli Palestinian conflict, and then, in the aftermath of 9/11, the Afghan and Iraq debacles. From one trouble spot to another, the Islamic Republic has managed to keep itself afloat over a sea of troubles, from economic to cultural, from national to regional, from domestic to global. The Islamic Republic has never, over the last three decades, been in a position of permanence or uncontested legitimacy, for suddenly to lose it over the last 6 months. The presidential election of June 2009 was just that proverbial straw that broke the camel's back. The color green eventually emerged as the campaign color of Mir-Hossein Mousavi's bid to become the Iranian president—and almost instantly fled into the varied mazes of Islamic, Iranian, and Persian sacred and mundane registers. It was, and it remains, multi-signatory. It signs, signals, and means many things. People love it for many reasons. The state hates it for only one reason. The state loses

67

patience and turns violent. People sing and dance in its shades and shadows. If a revolution, this is a revolt of unruly signs refusing to be incarcerated in dull and boring dictionaries.

This generation breaks all the rules. If you want to understand what is happening in the Green Movement, listen to the thunderous and defiant lyrics of the greatest Iranian rapper alive—Shahin Najafi. Look him up! Google him. You-Tube him. He has two Facebook pages. One was not enough for his fans. If Iranian cinema of the 1990s was the vision and vista of Khatami's Reform Movement, and Shahin Najafi's lyrics and music are the elegiac voice and loving fury of the Green Movement.

As the Islamic Republic had been managing its successive crisis one after another, a belligerent generation of oppositional figures and forces—now famously summarized in Pahlavi monarchists and MKO militarists—followed suit, not carefully choosing its enemies and effectively transmuted into them: undemocratic, dogmatic, cultic, frozen in a time zone beyond human reach. The Green Movement happened beyond the borders of banality and boredom that separate the Islamic Republic and its Opposition, hovering in a third space that gives life, liberty, and hope to those, the massive millions of them, beyond the reach of the closed society and its enemies.

The defining moment of this civil rights movement is its postideological disposition, marked by a massive generational gap that can only be explained by a demographic disposition that has capped a 72-million population with 80% of it under 40, 70% under 35, and 50% under 25. Predicated on this demography, and pushing the edges of what I must have learned by now about a country and clime I call home, my assessment of the Green Movement as a *civil rights movement* is not predicated on a sociological reading of its politics but marked by a political reading of its sociology. Let me explain. For over 200 years we Iranians have fought for the most fundamental institutions of a political modernity that has evaded our consistently colonial condition and persistently parasitical patrimonialism alike. The end result of that 200 years of struggle for political modernity has been the contorted character of the constitution of an Islamic Republic that in the precious words of the late Ayatollah Montazeri, the revered citizen-jurist, who has just posthumously been dubbed the moral voice of the Green Movement, is neither Islamic nor a republic.

With the constitution of the Islamic Republic, and particularly the undemocratic obscenity of its office of the supreme leader, my generation of Iranians hit a *cul de sac*. We had nowhere to go. The next generation of Iranians has now poured into the streets of their major and minor cities not with *our* habitual chants of "where is my gun," but with *their* strange but beautiful incantation of "where is my vote?" You may hear this generation chant, "I will kill, I will kill, he who killed my brother," but watch carefully for the instant a Basiji militiaman drops his helmet and finds himself in the middle of a chaotic embrace of streets and their claimants, men and women rush to have and hold him, pour water over his head to cool him off, kiss and cuddle him as a brother, as they rush to put a green scarf around his neck to make him one of their own.

The color green: it means you are a descendent of the prophet of Islam; and it means the poetry of Forough Farrokhzad, the poet laureate of our most cherished moments of solace and solitude:

> *I plant my hands in the small garden—*
> *I will grow green—*
> *I know*
> *I know*
> *I know*
> *And sparrows will nest and egg*
> *In the grooves*
> *In between my inky fingers*

These children you see roaming the streets of Iran with song and dance, they have all been hatched in those inky eggs our sister Forough planted in between her fingers inside that little garden. That is why they are all so green and beautiful.

Begun and continued as a civil rights movement, its color symbolism running ahead of its politics, this uprising has seen phases of civil disobedience and shades of civil unrest—but its skeletal vertebrae is a nonviolent drive toward democratic institutions that the current republic will either accommodate and survive, or else resist and be washed aside. The evident similarities between what we are witnessing now and what we did some 30 years ago should be carefully assayed—there are similarities, but not everything round is a walnut, as we say in Persian.

To the persistence of this civil rights movement the collapse of the Islamic Republic is almost irrelevant. The regime is collapsing from under the pressure of its own feeble constitution—a massive military industrial complex on one side and a simulacrum of republicanism on the other. The course of the civil rights movement is almost independent of that state apparatus, which may adapt to it and survive, or else resist it and be washed away. This movement will not die down and will only grow through the passage of time. There is no possible scenario that will divert it from its main objective—of reaching the goal of liberty, the rule of law, democratic republicanism, civil liberties, civil rights, women's rights, rights of the religious, and ethnic minorities.

Adapting to this movement and its unfolding demands for the Islamic Republic means one of three scenarios—in order of the desperation it faces: (1) dismantling the office of the supreme leader (*Velayat Faqih*) altogether but keeping the rest of the constitution intact, (2) reconvening a constitutional assembly to rewire a whole new constitution and put it to national vote; or else (3) discarding the very idea of an Islamic Republic altogether and putting the next form of the government to a plebiscite.

Against this inevitability, a number of scenarios might also be tempted to impose themselves: the most immediate is an open military coup by the Pasdaran; the second is a combination of US and or Israel-instigated economic embargo and military attack; the third is the internal implosion of the Islamic Republic followed by a militant takeover and hijacking of the uprising by such militant opposition forces as the MKO or (with the help of the United States and Israel military intervention) the monarchists, or a combination of both. All such possible scenarios have only one factor in common. They will categorically fail if they fail to recognize the nature of this movement as an inherently victorious, nonviolent, civil rights movement that will demand and exact civil liberties—freedom of expression, freedom of peaceful assembly, freedom to form political parties, and freedom to chose a democratic government.

The color green will remain the uncertain solace of this movement—no one will ever know what it exactly means—and that is a good thing. For it always means something contrary, something contrary to what the people in position of power thought it meant. It does not. It never does.

Notes

1. An earlier version of this essay was published as "Middle East is changed forever" in CNN.com (July 21, 2009).
2. An earlier version of this essay was published as "An Epistemic Shift in Iran" in *The Brooklyn Rail* (July–August 2009).

3. An earlier version of this essay was published as "Iran's democratic upsurge" in *al-Ahram Weekly* (18–24 June 2009).
4. An earlier version of this essay was published as "People Power" in *al-Ahram Weekly* (June 24 to July 1, 2009).
5. An earlier version of this essay was published in *New York Times* (June 23, 2009).
6. An earlier version of this essay was published as "Iran's Younger, Smarter Revolution" in *The Daily Beast* (January 2, 2010).

3

The Green Movement and Iran's Contemporary Political History

28-*Mordadism*: A Postmortem[1]

This year, Iranians around the world are commemorating the 56th anniversary of the CIA-sponsored coup of 1953, or as we call it indexically on Persian calendar, "*kudeta-ye 28 Mordad*." To that date we usually do not even add the year 1332 on our calendar, for just like 9/11, 28/Mordad has assumed such iconic significance that it is as if it happened in the Year Zero of our collective memory. In this essay, I wish to talk about the phenomenon of *28-Mordadism* as a political paradigm that peaked in modern Iranian political culture and has now finally exhausted itself.

For generations of Iranians, the coup of 1953 is not a mere historical event. It is the most defining moment of their lives, for it is the most haunting national trauma of their modern history—of foreign intervention followed by domestic tyranny. Iranians cannot speak of 28-*Mordad* without a certain raw nerve suddenly springing up and about entirely involuntarily. The first thing that Iranians do when they speak of 28-Mordad is to remember a personal story, where they were and what they were doing, very much like the assassination of John F. Kennedy (on November 22, 1963), or Malcolm X (on February 21, 1965), or MLK Jr. (on April 4, 1968) for Americans. When it happened something died and something else came to life. *28-Mordadism* is the central trope of modern Iranian historiography.

The posttraumatic syndrome of the coup of 1953 was best summed up and captured in "Zemestan/Winter" (1955), now the legendary poem of Mehdi Akhavan Sales (1928–1990). "No one returns your greetings/Heads are dropped deeply into collars," became the talismanic opening of a poem that defined an entire generation of fear and loathing, self-imposed solitude and forsaken hopes. Akhavan Sales' other poems, "Marsiyeh/Requiem," "Shahryar Shar-e Sangestan/ the Prince of Stoneville," "Chavoshi/Ballad," etc. were all written and read as lachrymal melodies for what could have or might have been but was not. When in 1978, Akhavan Sales' "Marsiyeh/Requiem" gave Amir Naderi the inspiration for his dark foreboding of the revolution to come in his namesake feature film *Marsiyeh/Requiem* (1978), soon after he made the epic opposite of it *Tangsir* (1974), the coup of 1953 was running quietly through the heart of Pahlavi regime in two opposing directions—quiet desperation and euphoric hope. Between Amir Naderi's *Tangsir* and *Marsiyeh*, we might say, or between Ahmad Shamlou's defiant cry for freedom and Mehdi Akhavan Sales' painful dwellings on our lost future in our nostalgic past, or living in the middle of Forough Farrokhzad's poem *Kasi keh Mesl-e Hich Kas Nist* or *Someone who is like no one* and Sohrab Sepehri's *Seda ye pa-ye Ab or Sounds of Footsteps of water*, an entire nation born and raised in the aftermath of the coup of 1953 learned how to oscillate between depths of despair and ecstatic visions of hope.

By now we had become bi-polar in our schizophrenic remembrances of 28-Mordad. Thus *28-Mordadism*, as if absorbing all our history in one sound byte, felt like the birth pangs of delivery into an overwhelming awareness of our colonial modernity, of not being in charge of our own destiny, of everything that was best in us collapsing into mere phantom liberties, devoid of substance, of material basis, of formative force, of moral authority.

On the political stage, not just everything that occurred *after* 28-Mordad but even things that have happened *before* it suddenly came together to posit the phenomenon of 28-Mordadism: foreign intervention, colonial domination, imperial arrogance, domestic tyranny, an "enemy" always lurking behind a corner to come and rob us of our liberties, of a mere possibility of democratic institutions. The result has been a categorical circumlocution—at once debilitating and enabling—that begins with the Tobacco Revolt of 1890–1892, runs through the Constitutional Revolution of 1906–1911, and concludes with the Islamic Revolution of 1979. Under the colonial condition that has originally occasioned this mental state of siege and enabled it to spin around itself, we have lived through a persistent politics of *force major* in which we have placed the forceful substitution of a *revolutionary expediency* in lieu of a *public reason*.

I believe that the June 2009 presidential election marks an epistemic exhaustion of *28-Mordadism*, when the paradigm has conjugated itself *ad nauseum* and in the most recent rendition of it by the custodians of the Islamic Republic, best represented in the Public Prosecutor's indictment against hundreds of reformists, has in fact degenerated into a political Tourette Syndrome, whereby an evidently psychotic political disorder has begun to tic involuntarily, with vile and violent exclamations of coprolalia. The Islamic Republic carrying *28-Mordadism ad nauseum* is coterminous with an epistemic passage beyond it at the more commanding level of the Iranian political culture, a discursive sublimation that is predicated on a crucial closure of a posttraumatic syndrome that commenced soon after the 1953 coup and concluded in the course of the Islamic Revolution of 1977–1979.

The traumatic memory of the coup of 1953 was very much rekindled and put to very effective political use in the most crucial episodes of the nascent Islamic Republic in order to consolidate its fragile foundations.

When on February 1, 1979 Ayatollah Khomeini returned to Iran, soon after the Shah had left, the idea of an Islamic Republic was far from certain and there was an array of political positions and forces ranging from nationalist to socialist to Islamist. In the period March 30–31, Khomeini ordered a national referendum, and on April 1, he declared that the Islamic Republic had been overwhelmingly endorsed and established. But by no stretch of the imagination was this referendum convincing to major segments of the political and intellectual elite or the population at large, for which reason, as early as June, Khomeini was lashing out against what he termed "Westoxicated intellectuals." By mid-June, the official draft of the constitution of the Islamic Republic was published. But there was no mention of any *Velayat-e Faqih* in it. Khomeini endorsed this draft, as he continued his attacks against the "Westoxicated intellectuals," who at this point were actively demanding the formation of a *Majles-e Moassessan* or a Constitutional Assembly to examine the terms of the constitution. (I was present in one such meeting in Tehran University in July 1979.) Khomeini openly opposed this idea and announced that there will be "no Westernized jurists" writing any constitution for the Islamic Republic—"only the noble clergy." Meanwhile Khomeini's doctrine of *Velayat-e Faqih* was being actively disseminated in the country. By early August, *Ayandegan* newspaper, which was actively questioning the notion of *Velayat-e Faqih* was savagely attacked by the Islamist vigilantes and then officially banned.

At the same time a major National Democratic Front rally at Tehran University soccer field was viciously attacked (I was present in this rally). By mid-August, the Assembly of Experts had gathered to write the constitution of the Islamic Republic, and by mid-October they had completed their deliberations and drafted the constitution, with the office of *Vali Faqih* in it.

The constitution of the Islamic Republic was written under conditions that there were both intellectual and militant opposition to it, and Khomeini's circle was in a warring pose to consolidate and institutionalize it at all cost. A perfect opportunity was given to them when on October 22 the late Shah came to the United States for cancer treatment, which Khomeini instantly called a plot and invoked the memory of 1953 to make it credible. When on November 1 the liberal Mehdi Bazargan was pictured shaking hands with Zbigniew Brzezinski in Algeria, not just the Islamists but even the left thought that the Americans were on to something again. Iranians were bitten by a snake in 1953, as we say in Persian, so they were afraid of any black or white rope.

The American Hostage Crisis began on November 4, 1979, lasted 444 days, and by the time it ended on January 20, 1981, it had used and abused the memory of the 1953 coup to consolidate the fragile foundations of an Islamic theocracy. Two days after the hostages were taken, the weak and wobbly Bazargan was pushed aside and forced to resign. The militant Islamists assumed a warring posture. They were now fighting the Great Satan, and the left and the liberals, the fainthearted and the soft-spoken, better stay clear of the fight. Exactly in this atmosphere, on December 2, Khomeini ordered the newly prepared constitution of the Islamic Republic put to vote and then reported that it was massively approved, and he became the supreme leader. Soon after that, on January 25, 1980, the first presidential election of the Islamic Republic was conducted and Bani Sadr was declared its winner. Soon after that, on March 15 the first parliamentary election was held, with Hezbollah vigilantes attacking the headquarters of all surviving opposition parties, especially the Mojahedin-e Khalq Organization, dismantling and discrediting them so that they would not be part of the parliament. That was not enough. On March 21, the eve of the Persian New Year, Khomeini ordered the "cultural revolution," and thus commenced the militant Islamization of the universities by the intellectual echelon among his devotee (some of them now the leading oppositional intellectuals). All of these crucial steps toward the radical Islamization of the Iranian Revolution (and with its political culture) were done under the *force major* of a repetition of 1953—*28-Mordadism* at its height.

As if Khomeini needed another excuse to prove that a US plot against the revolution was in the offing, on April 25, Operation Eagle Claw to rescue the American hostages met with a catastrophic and (for President Jimmy carter) embarrassing and costly end in the Iranian deserts, providing further fuel and momentum to Khomeini's revolutionary zeal, so that during the following May, June, and July further Islamization of the state bureaucracy took place, purging anyone suspected of not being committed to the revolution. This in effect amounted to the mass expulsion of Iranians suspected of ideological impurity from the state apparatus. The same story was repeated after the July 11 Nojeh coup attempt, which fueled Khomeini's fury even more, resulting in the persecution of alternative voices and movements and the radical Islamization of the revolution—the shadow of 1953 was kept consciously, deliberately, and successfully on the horizon.

Finally on July 27 Shah died in Egypt and the American hostages began to lose their usefulness to Khomeini; and when on 22 September Saddam Hussein invaded Iran and the 8-day grueling Iran–Iraq War started, the hostage crisis had completely performed its strategic function as a smoke screen for Khomeini's radical Islamization of the revolution and the brutal elimination of all alternative forces and voices. By October 26, Iraqi forces had entered Iran and occupied Khorram-Shahr, and Iran was fully engaged in a deadly war with Iraq. On January 20, 1981, Khomeini allowed the American hostages to be released, and shifted his attention to the Iran–Iraq War, under which more domestic suppression, and more radical Islamization of the Iranian political culture, society, and above all historiography took place.

With the commencement of the Reform movement in late 1990s, *28-Mordadism* began losing its grip on Iranian political culture, after decades of abusing it to sustain an otherwise illegitimate state apparatus. At the moment, custodians of the Islamic Republic continue to abuse it—but for all intents and purposes, the paradigm has now completely exhausted itself, hit a plateau, well passed the point of its diminishing return. The end of *28-Mordadism* of course does not mean the end of imperial interventions in the historical destiny of nations. It just means that we have a renewed and level playing field to think and act in postcolonial terms.

Return of the Repressed[2]

Thirty-one years after the 1979 Revolution, Iranians are up and about revolting against yet another illegitimate government and challenging the rule of yet another tyrannical regime.

In a key passage, in a recent interview that Mir-Hossein Mousavi, the oppositional candidate now spearheading the Green Movement, had given in anticipation of the 31st anniversary of the 1979 Revolution, has said that early in the course of that momentous uprising the majority of Iranians were convinced that dictatorship had ended in Iran. "I was one of those people," he then added. "But today I no longer believe that to be the case."

Today, he observed, we can see both the signs of dictatorship and the resistance to that dictatorship. He then claimed this resistance as a legacy of the Islamic Revolution. "It must be said," he stipulates, "that people's resistance is a heritage of the Islamic Revolution. People's discontent with deceit, deception, and corruption, which we witness today, are among the clear signs of this heritage."

There is an evident logical fallacy in Mr. Mousavi's claiming the current uprising in Iran for civil liberties as a direct legacy of the Islamic Revolution. If the courage and imagination that Iranians are showing in this civil rights moment are caused by the Islamic Revolution, then what causes the Islamic Revolution in the first place?

The modern Iranian history did not begin with that brutally Islamized revolution. The same collective sentiments and the same multifaceted political culture that caused the 1979 revolution in the first place, and that has been systematically suppressed for over three decades, has now come back to torment its tormentors.

Mr. Mousavi is 68 years old. When 30 years ago he joined the rank of the revolutionaries in the course of the 1977–1979 revolution he was himself a grown man and a committed Islamist that knew only too well the competing ideas and aspirations that moved and mobilized his people. The militant Islamism of the 1970s was integral, but by no means definitive, to a vast, rich, and diversified political culture in which anticolonial nationalism and Third World socialism were equally if not more integral.

That cosmopolitan political culture was in the making long before the Islamized revolution had came about as yet another critical moment in the tireless history of a people and their steady march toward freedom. The young Iranians pouring into the streets of their homeland today to demand and soon to exact their civil liberties are nourished, moved, and inspired by the same fountain of liberty that had moved their parents, which the Islamic Republic, for 8 crucial years under the steady hand of Mr. Mousavi himself, had brutally repressed.

What we are witnessing in the streets of Iran and among Iranians around the globe is the resurgence of the Iranian cosmopolitan political culture that caused and conditioned their 1979 revolution, and that has been violently eclipsed under the violent absolutism of a militant Islamism that is institutionalized in a fundamentally flawed republic and a thinly disguised theocracy.

The history of the Islamic Republic over the last three decades has been a sad and sullied scenario of suppression and brutality, the apparition of a state apparatus disguising the fact of a guerrilla operation mis/managing one crisis after another, some of which it creates as diversionary tactics, and others have come its way by the follies of powers and superpowers in its immediate and distant neighborhood, and that have been windblown treasures for its abusive opportunism.

The Iranian Revolution of 1977–1979 was a magnificent manifestation of the multifaceted and polyfocal Iranian political culture against a tyrannical monarchy in which anticolonial nationalism, grassroot socialism, as well as militant Islamism had a fair and balanced share. The American Hostage Crisis of 1979–1980 was the first manufactured crisis that militant Islamists created as a smoke screen to divert the world attention while they went on a rampage and took an entire political culture hostage to their single-mindedly Islamist take on a cosmopolitan culture.

The American Hostage crisis had not ended yet, when the Iran–Iraq War (1980–1988) started, and with it there was yet another prolonged and brutal distraction that Ayatollah Khomeini used to eliminate all his internal oppositions. He did not start the war with Iraq. Saddam Hossein did, with the full support of the Reagan administration and its European and Arab allies. But Khomeini prolonged it for his own internal and regional reasons.

Two years into the Iran–Iraq War, the Israelis invaded Lebanon in 1982 and offered the Islamic Republic the best opportunity to help create the Lebanese Hezbollah and extend its regional power base. The Iran–Iraq War was still raging apace when the commencement of the First Intifada (1987–1993) provided the Islamic Republic with yet another opportunity to expand its presence in occupied Palestine.

The Iran–Iraq War had barely ended when Saddam Hossein invaded Kuwait, the Taliban took over Afghanistan, and the two monsters, the

79

United States and its European, regional, and Arab allies had created to control the spread of the Iranian Rrevolution came back to haunt them all and turn against their own creators.

The tragic events of 9/11 plunged the United States into a deep quagmire of mismanaging one crisis after another of its own making in Afghanistan and Iraq, as the Israeli invasion of Lebanon in 2006 and Gaza in 2008–2009 added more fuel to the fire ablaze among Arabs and Muslims—and by every turn of the screw and as the United States was being bugged down in the region, the Islamic Republic was busy doing what it has always done best: taking advantage of one crisis after another in the region to stay afloat and disguise its fundamentally turbulent claim to legitimacy among its own citizens.

Thirty years into the brutal manufacturing of an Islamist state and its forceful imposition on an open-minded, vastly worldly, highly educated, deeply cultivated, and constitutionally multicultural people, the Green Movement has emerged from the very depths of Iranian political culture to surpass and transcend any exclusionary and absolutist claim on it.

Today the Green Movement is threatened by a number of divergent factors and forces. A brutal suppression by the security apparatus of the Islamic Republic is only the most immediate and evident threat. Equally dangerous to its fundamental aspirations is any neoconservative delusion that this movement is to liberate Iran and make it safe for a neoliberal economics that can scarce generate and sustain jobs in the United States, let alone export itself around the globe. Thus, to save the Green Movement from its supporters among the American Think Tanks from Washington DC to Stanford, California, it is still good to read Mir-Hossein Mousavi invoking the memory of a vast social revolution that had a fundamental commitment to social and economic justice at the heart of its historic moment.

Notes

1. An earlier version of this essay was published by the *Tehran Bureau* (December 3, 2009).
2. An earlier version of this essay was published as "Repressed voices speak out in Iran" in CNN.com (February 10, 2010).

4

Legitimacy Challenges to the "Islamic Republic"

The Islamic Republic is Self-Destructing[1]

*Ma bi-shomarim/*We are countless.

A slogan of the Green Movement in Iran

Within minutes after the picture of a frail and fragile Mohammad Ali Abtahi appeared on the Internet, the blogosphere was flooded with split images of him before and after his predicament. Having lost some 20 kilos since his incarcerations in late June, his handsome, ever-smiling and endearing face thinned beyond recognition, disrobed of his clerical habit, his turban lost, and clad in an unseemly prison pajama, the former vice president under president Mohammad Khatami (1997–2005), a leading reformist, and particularly popular with bloggers because of his own Weblog, Abtahi's case was particularly heart-wrenching to his young admirers. The belligerent custodians of the Islamic Republic had forced him to confess to crimes that made a dead chicken laugh, as we say in Persian, and as an oppositional figure quickly pointed out. This is a velvet revolution, he was made to say, plotted by the reformists, supported by the "Enemy," and there was nothing wrong with Ahmadinejad's landslide victory. Instead of sadness and disappointment, the blogosphere was abuzz with love and admiration for Abtahi. He was instantly declared a national hero. "For the first time," said one blogger, "I learned to love a cleric—and then I looked again, he had no clerical robe anymore." Mohsen Makhmalbaf, the leading Iranian filmmaker now active in support of the Green Movement delivered the most memorable punch line in support of Abtahi, dismissing his forced confessions. "If Khamenei were to be treated like Abtahi in jail, the supreme leader would come to national television and do belly dancing!"

Every state is founded on force, Max Weber believed early in the twentieth century. What Weber termed "legitimate violence," as the defining apparatus of any state, is predicated on what he called "external means" and "inner justification." The more a state has to resort to external means (use of violence), the less its claim on any inner justification (constitutional mandates) on part of its citizens.

The massively orchestrated and naked violence that the Islamic Republic has launched against its own citizens (young and old, men and women, rich and poor) has not only delegitimized its claim on any notion of a "republic," it has, ipso facto, discredited any claim to "Islam" that it may have—or even in more troubling terms, it is bordering with discrediting Islam itself, which is the reason why so many prominent, high-ranking, Shi'i clerics are coming out so forcefully and categorically denouncing the violent crackdown of peaceful demonstrations, in both juridical and rational terms. There were many Iranians who doubted the accuracy of the June presidential election results; and there were those who thought they were perfectly accurate. But the vicious, blatantly criminal, activities of people in position of power in the Islamic Republic have now assumed a reality sui generis, beyond anything that any critic of this election had ever uttered. The Islamic Republic is self-destructing.

Over the last 2 months, scores of innocent young Iranians have been cold-bloodedly murdered, either in the streets or else under torture in the dungeons of the Islamic Republic. Amnesty International, Human Rights Watch, and the International Campaign for Human Rights in Iran, three different and autonomous human rights organizations, have independently documented and condemned atrocious acts of human rights abuse—of arbitrary arrests, kidnappings, illegal incarceration, indiscriminate beating and torture, and the cold-blooded murder of ordinary citizens. To the haunted names of Abu Ghraib, Guantanamo Bay, Bagram Airbase, and even Gulag now has to be added the dreaded names of Kahrizak and Evin, as the sites of appalling atrocities perpetrated by the security apparatus of a self-consciously illegitimate tyranny. Never will any official of the Islamic Republic be able to utter a word about the criminal behaviors of the US army in Iraq or the equally atrocious acts of the Israeli army in Palestine with a straight face and without *ipso facto* implicating their own atrocities against their own innocent citizens. Mehdi Karroubi, a leading oppositional figure, recently said, even the Zionists (for their proverbial brutalities against the Palestinians) behave with more self-restraint in Gaza than the Iranian security apparatus does against its own citizens. The horrors of the Islamic Republic do not whitewash the terrors that the Jewish state perpetrates against Palestinians in their own homeland. They underline them. Ahmadinejad has no moral voice to point a finger at Israel. The dead bodies of Neda Aqa Soltan, Sohrab A'rabi, and scores of other young Iranians murdered at the prime of their lives are.

The security apparatus of the Islamic Republic behaves like a wild beast, chasing after its own tail, maiming and murdering anyone in its way. Innocent citizens are arbitrarily arrested, or, worse, kidnapped off the streets (like the prominent human rights lawyer Shadi Sadr), incarcerated in their hundreds, at times viciously tortured, or even cold-bloodedly murdered, and their bodies given to their families on the condition that they utter no word of protest and bury their loved ones quietly. Leading public intellectuals, political activists, reformist journalists, university professors, and political analysts are arrested, charged with treason, forced to confess to outlandish charges, and then paraded in front of national television in kangaroo courts to humiliate and break them in the public eye. Anyone with a smidgeon of intelligence, a caring intellect, a moral fiber in their being is suspect.

It took 30 years of an Islamic Republic to cleanse it of its innate banalities and to produce a leading cadre of public intellectuals who deeply care about their people, love their country, abide by the law of their land, and with a perfectly legitimate range of positions and opinions on social and economic matters, wish to work for a better future—and it took exactly that many years for yet another genera-tion of opportunist charlatans to gather around Ali Khamenei and Mahmoud Ahmadinejad to kill (like a number of public intellectuals in the late 1990s), paralyze (like the chief reformist strategist Said Haj-jarian), force into exile (like Abdolkarim Soroush, Mohsen Kadivar, Akbar Ganji, Mohsen Makhmalbaf, or Ata Mohajerani), incarcerate, torture, humiliate, discredit, or kill (too numerous to name) anyone who dares to speak truth to the powers that be. That intellectual elite is systematically eradicated, murdered, incarcerated, discredited, forced into exile in order to pave the ignominious path of a medieval banality codenamed *Velayat-e Faqih*, a keyword for the rule of fear and fanaticism, structural ignorance, and religious fascism. *Farhang-e Nokhbeh-koshi* or the Culture of Eliticide is what one perceptive Iranian analyst has called this dark urge of tyranny.

83

Meanwhile, whatever has survived of this eliticide and gathered around an innocuous but hopeful green color to codify an unprecedented civil rights movement is now the target of even harsher attacks by a certain quixotic side of the expatriate "opposition," who discredit anyone who might harbor a smidgeon of hope for the future. They do nothing but malign any public figure that this movement has chosen as its leaders. Much legitimate anger lingers in their prose, degenerating though into an illegitimate malignancy of moral retardation and political impotence. What they offer instead is the moldy residues of old apothecary boxes of clichés, locked in their mind and soul in some Neanderthal age of convictions, without an iota of critical or creative intelligence about them. They are a sorry and sad scene: much coarsened convictions and yet not an iota of hope, of trust, of crossing the psychological barrier of getting muddied with the nuts and bolts of a magnificent civil rights movement that belongs to no one in particular and is in need of every ounce of creative intelligence that comes to its aid.

These noises notwithstanding, the central volume of the movement is crystal clear and rising. The Green Movement does not belong to anyone. From Mir-Hossein Mousavi inside Iran to Reza Pahlavi and Masoud Rajavi of the Mojahedin-e Khalq outside lay a claim to it. But in and of itself, it moves like a beautiful river, self-propelling, like Hudson or Karun, now thunderous and dangerous, now calm and quiet. Fortunately no charismatic rabble-rouser has any legitimate claim to it. The most significant dimension of this movement is its historic transvaluation of values, its categorical denunciation of violence in the face of ungodly violence that seeks to put an end to it. It will not.

The belligerent custodians of the Islamic Republic capture and torture Mohammad Abtahi, and force him to come and confess to bogus charges on national television, and yet within hours masses of e-mails and Weblogs shower him with love and forgiveness, understanding and tolerance, and hope and happiness. The Islamic Republic wants to humiliate Abtahi; people turn him into a national hero and publish thousands of "confessions" of a similar sort to make him feel better and to express their love for and solidarity with him.

Putting their lives and liberties on the line are not just ordinary citizens and their extraordinary courage and imagination. The most learned juridical authorities of the land, high-ranking Shi'i clerics, from Ayatollah Montazeri to Ayatollah Sane'i, to Hojjat al-Islam Mohsen Kadivar, reminiscent in their courage and conviction of the best that the Constitutional Revolution of 1906–1911 had produced, have gone public denouncing these naked brutalities of the Islamic Republic. One of the most distinguished Shi'is scholars of the land, Seyyed Mostafa Mohaqqeq Damad, in an open letter to Ayatollah Hashemi Shahroudi, the Head of the Judiciary, denounced the absurd kangaroo courts that has robbed innocent citizens of their rights and speaks to the highest juridical authority of the land not as a jurist but "as a citizen." These are groundbreaking moments in modern Iranian history, and it will leave no stone unturned in its neighborhood.

The Islamic Republic may die a quick death or else suffer ignominy through a slow demise—that will be determined not by its unending brutalities but by the grace and pace of a civil rights movement that is changing the moral map of this godforsaken term we gave inherited from our colonial past—"the Middle East." The rise and demise of the Islamic Republic follows the simple law of diminishing return—there is only so much abuse that a people can take, or an outdated idea can exercise. After that, the more abuse you heap on a people the less effective it becomes. For 30 years, the Islamic Republic violently distorted a multifaceted cosmopolitan political culture and crudely cut and shoved its limbs inside a medieval juridical apothecary box, and to suppress and silence its own people assumed a warring posture against regional atrocities of entirely different origin and destination. If Iraq is in shambles, Palestine is brutalized, Afghanistan is marred by highway bandits and supersonic bombers, and none of these calamities justifies the banalities of an Islamic Republic that has abused them for far too long to be able to continue to justify its parasitical persistence.

Today the Islamic Republic has finally outsmarted itself and hit the plateau of diminishing return, where its opportunist warring postures in the region can no longer hide the horrors of its own criminal theocracy. This point of diminishing return is where all tyrannies ultimately end. It is not just the Islamic Republic that has finally outsmarted itself and is beginning to self-destruct. The same fate awaited George W. Bush and the Christian Empire he sought to build, and where the American military and material wherewithal could not afford such imperial largesse and began to unfold in both Afghanistan and Iraq. The Islamic Republic is self-destructing because it played its transparent hand for too long and too clumsily, precisely the same way that the Jewish state has played its victimhood for too long and too clumsily. Nobody could defeat Zionism, so Zionism defeated itself, by being too arrogant, too indulgent, and too brazen in its disregard for basic human decency—thinking it could just wipe Palestine and Palestinians off the face of the map. Well—Palestinians were not wiped off the face of the map. They are still there, and they are fighting back—tall, towering, and erect. But belligerent Zionism, just like militant Islamism, and just like Christian and Hindu fundamentalism, has morally run aground. The Israeli 2006 invasion of Lebanon and then the 2008–2009 massacre of Palestinians in Gaza were the ultimate signs of its moral and military meltdown, its naked brutalities exposing the fact that it too, just like its Islamist counterpart in Iran, had hit the point of diminishing return, where people no longer buy its outworn commodification of victimhood, as best documented and argued by Norman Finkelstein.

The dawn of a new beginning is brightly upon us—not just in Iran, but in the entire region. The nonviolent civil rights movement in Iran is changing the moral map of the region, its normative vocabulary, its visions, vistas, and prospects of itself. It crosses over Sunni-Shi'i divide, Arab–Persian racism, Arab–Israel conflict, religious–secular chasm, and bridges over much troubled and muddied water. To mark my point, here is a passage from a Persian blog by a young Iranian blogger that I quote here to salute my distinguished Israeli detractor who calls me typically "Persian and emotional":

> In the history books of the 21st century, the first chapter will be about us. In the introduction, they might write that important events have happened before us, events like 9/11 and war on Iraq and Afghanistan, but those were the remnants of the previous century, with an outdated language and with Twentieth century tools: Airplanes, bombs and bullets. And then they will write that the first chapter is dedicated to us because we have been the true children of our time ... They will write that we were the first social movement that all of us were its leader and all of us were its organizer... They may make a subsection to describe how a movement without a command center was acting so well-orchestrated. How its ideas, desires, and slogans were suggested, criticized, and completed so well, and then one day they were expressed in such a harmony as if all these millions had practiced them together for years... In the same chapter they will write that we lived the last days of guns and bullets and we showed that where awareness, information, and channels of communication for human connection exist, bullets are pointless. They may put a picture of a single bullet somewhere in our Freedom Museum and write for its caption "the last bullet that was ever pulled out of a magazine."

The Moral Meltdown of the Islamic Republic[2]

Troubling news of kidnapping, rape, torture, and murder is flooding out of Iran. Neda Aqa Soltan was murdered point blank in the streets of Tehran for the whole world to watch; while Sohrab Arabi was killed far from any global attention, and his dead body was given to his mother quietly to bury, as was the tortured and dead body of Mohsen Ruholamini. These names have assumed symbolic significance for many more innocent young men and women murdered by the custodians of the Islamic Republic with a wanton disregard for the lives and liberties of its own citizens.

Not just murder, but also raping of young men and women is now on the shameless roster of the Islamic Republic. After years of sporadic charges and troubling rumors, finally a courageous cleric has put a stamp of public recognition on atrocious practices in the theocratic state. One of the revolutionary founders of the Islamic Republic, who is a high-ranking cleric, a presidential candidate, a former Speaker of the House, and now a widely popular political activist, Mehdi Karroubi has published a letter in which he accuses the security officers of the Islamic Republic of repeatedly and violently raping young women and men while in their custody. Since the publication of this letter, a massive outpour of testimonies and reports are coming out corroborating Karroubi's charges that widespread raping of young women and men has been a common practice in the Islamic Republic.

These are not light charges for any state, for any republic, let alone for an Islamic Republic. These charges are no longer brought by expatriate, and at times discredited, opposition. It is the founding fathers of the Islamic Republic, with impeccable revolutionary credentials, who are bringing these charges, insist on them, as others are coming out and corroborating them in excruciating details. The Islamic Republic has never faced such a deep crisis of legitimacy in its 30-year turbulent history.

As widely evident, today it is not just the "republican" claim of the regime that is in question and in fact in jeopardy; but, perhaps far more seriously, it is its claim to Islam that has troubling consequences for more than 1.3 billion Muslims around the world. People in the streets of Tehran are chanting, paraphrasing a famous slogan of the 1979 revolution, "independence, freedom, Iranian Republic," pointedly replacing "Iranian" for "Islamic." Though a perfectly legitimate demand, by no means is this is a common denominator among the growing opposition to the regime. To the degree that at least in part he represents this uprising, Mir-Hossein Mousavi, as a pious and practicing Muslim, continues to insist that he wishes to restore the ideals and aspirations of the Islamic Revolution within the constitution of the state.

What we are witnessing in Iran today are two contradictory signs of the relationship between Islam and democracy. Never have the two opposing ideas of an "Islamic Republic," and Muslims living in a democratic Republic been so evidently at odds with each other. The 30-year experience of the Islamic Republic shows fundamental flaws in the ideals and aspirations of defining a state apparatus in the exclusive terms of a militantly juridical Islam, while at the same time Iranians, the overwhelming majority of them Shiite Muslims, have repeatedly demonstrated, under this very regime, that they are perfectly capable of a democratic behavior. Not just as immigrants in EU and the United States, but as citizens in Iran, millions of Muslims have demonstrated that they are integral to the democratic institutions embedded in the very notion of a nation-state.

Like Jews, Christians, or Hindus, Muslims are perfectly capable of living in and helping sustain a democracy. What is in question is the viability of an Islamic Republic, a Jewish State, a Christian Empire, or a Hindu fundamentalism. As in the rest of the Muslim world, Islam is of course integral to Iranian society but not definitive to it. Over the last 30 years a radically juridical interpretation of a cosmopolitan faith has been force-fed into a multifaceted political culture—and today the violent convulsion of the system is for the whole world to see. There has been much talk of the need for an Islamic "reformation" over the last few years. What Islam needs is no Christian-style reformation. What Islam needs is a *restoration* of its historically cosmopolitan character in which non-Muslims lived in peace and prosperity, and which they now need to retrieve in order to live in peace and prosperity in a non-entirely Muslim world.

By virtue of living in a democracy, and having endured indignities of rampant Islamophobia in their own country, American Muslims have an extraordinarily historic role to play, by way of sending a delegation to Iran, connecting to this grassroots democratic movement in a Muslin nation, and helping it restore its cosmopolitan character in its pursuit of enduring democratic institutions.

The Crisis of an Islamic Republic[3]

THESE are the times that try men's souls ... Tyranny, like hell, is not easily conquered; yet we have this consolation with us, that the harder the conflict, the more glorious the triumph. What we obtain too cheap, we esteem too lightly: it is dearness only that gives every thing its value. Heaven knows how to put a proper price upon its goods; and it would be strange indeed if so celestial an article as FREEDOM should not be highly rated.

Thomas Paine, *The American Crisis* (1776)

The Islamic Revolution (1977–1979) began by a concerted mobilization of political forces against the Pahlavi dynasty and succeeded to establish an Islamic Republic after a violent distortion of Iranian polity. The diverse aspects of Iranian political culture not compatible with a militant Islamist take of Ayatollah Khomeini were brutally and systematically eliminated. This worldly polity was and remains too cosmopolitan to be coded simply as "secular." Militant secularists are distorting the multifaceted Iranian political culture and are distorting Iranian political culture precisely in the same violent ways that the militant Islamists do. Thirty years after the forced-fed over-Islamization of the Iranian cosmopolitan culture, a new generation of public intellectuals, political and social leaders, human and civil rights activists emerged from the very bosom of the Islamic Republic, demanding their civil liberties and wishing to correct the course of an Islamic Republic they saw had gone terribly wrong. These liberties, they finally realized, are not only constitutional to any notion of a *republic* to which the Islamic Republic seems to have a claim but also coterminous with the multifaceted Iranian political culture that was systematically violated in order to make that Islamic Republic possible. The crisis of legitimacy that has now finally caught up with the Islamic Republic is not only evident in its vile and violent behavior toward its own citizens but in fact coterminous with its very existence. Some 30 years after its violent crackdown of all its alternatives, this crisis is now not merely political but infinitely more pointedly moral—going deeply into the very heart of the very idea of an "Islamic" Republic.

The forced transmutation of Iranian political culture into a singularly Islamic site was an act of epistemic violence that could only be sustained by a militarized security apparatus that forced its intellectual and political oppositions into exile or else brutally eliminated them. But the Islamic Republic could not uproot and transform Iranian society at large, and from the older roots of the selfsame political culture new branches have sprouted out—wiser, sharper, stronger, and more intelligent than their parental generation. Iranian civil society and political culture are not just ahead of its backward and retrograde leaders but also equally ahead of their stilted intellectuals—trapped inside a number of binary opposition: in or out of Iran, left or right, religious or otherwise. The civil rights movement that has finally broken out in the aftermath of the June 12th presidential election is reducible to neither side of any such false binary—for it is, ipso facto, reaching out to retrieve the Iranian cosmopolitan culture, to which Islam is integral, but not definitive. Unless we come to terms with the worldly disposition of that cosmopolitan culture, the nature of the crisis that the Islamic Republic faces, or the civil rights movement that has now ensued, will not make sense or critically register.

After Mehdi Karroubi, a founding member of the Islamic Republic and an aging revolutionary, as well as others, disclosed that young Iranians are being raped and murdered in the dungeons of the Islamic Republic, and then hurriedly buried in mass graves, something far more crucial than the "republican" claim of the Islamic Republic being in jeopardy—it was its claim on Islam, and thus *Islam itself* that had to run for cover. After violently denying, denigrating, destroying, forcing into exile, or seeking to discredit the non-Islamist dimensions of Iranian cosmopolitan culture—ranging from anticolonial nationalist to Third World socialist in its political registers—the Islamic Republic placed all its legitimate eggs in one Islamic basket. Once that basket was dropped on the hard surface of mass graves in Behesht-e Zahra cemetery, burying scores of young Iranians cold-bloodedly murdered because of their political positions, or simply for having voted for one presidential candidate as opposed to another, the Islamic Republic was pulling Islam down to its grave too. It is now Islam, the faith of millions of Iranians and other human beings that must survive the banality of this particular evil.

To retrieve the cosmopolitan culture of Iran, with the rightful and democratic place of Islam in it, we have absolutely no choice but to think of ways to reduce the magnitude of violence that is unleashed upon us, that is unleashed upon the world in our name, first and foremost by not falling into its trap and reciprocating it. Violence is violence and violence must be condemned—genocidal, homicidal, or suicidal. The Israeli genocidal violence against Palestinians does not justify Palestinian suicidal violence against Israelis—it just exacerbates it. American homicidal violence in Afghanistan and Iraq does not justify Afghan or Iraqi suicidal violence either—it just extends its madness. Muslims, Jews, Christians, and Hindus are today at each other's throat. We have inherited a politics of despair that has reduced us to desperate measures. In revenge to what the world has done to Afghanistan, it is as if the whole world is being reduced to Afghanistan—a disparate people desperately in search of an illusive peace, robbed of their dignity, commanding culture, sustained civility, moral whereabouts, and at the mercy of drug traffickers, highway bandits, and supersonic bombers alike.

Iran is today ruled by a criminal band of militant Taliban look-alikes—savagely beating, raping, torturing, and point blank murdering the people they are suppose to protect. They are, as Mehdi Karroubi once famously put it, worse than Zionists, for the Zionists do what they do to Palestinians, not to Israelis. The answer to that kind of indiscriminate violence cannot be violence, for it will plunge us all into even deeper layers of hell that is now code-named "the Islamic Republic."

A *Nakba* of no less catastrophic consequence than that of the Palestinians, though perpetrated against now more than 72 million people, is casting its deadly and languorous shadow over an entire nation. A worldly cosmopolitan culture has been reduced to a narrowly exacting Shi'i juridicalism and the tongue-twisting legalese of a fraternity club that insists on speaking their clerically inflected Persian with Latinate obscurantism written into its very diction. Perfectly beautiful Arabic words, such as *Tanfidh* and *Tahlif*, are clumsily thrown at Persian syntax and morphology and made to look and sound strange and self-alienating in Persian when uttered by the clerically inflected obscurantism of a band of clerics who think Iran is their paternal inheritance and we ordinary folks are just a nuisance that ought to be regulated in the sanctified letters of their law.

In this regard, it really makes no difference how progressive or retrograde a *Faqih* is—for they are identical in their excessive *fiqhification* of Iranian political culture. The only reason, as a result, that such prominent clerical figures as Ayatollah Montazeri, Ayatollah Sane'i, or Hojjat al-Islam Kadivar are dearer to us than others is because they declare themselves and do their best (and sometime they succeed) to speak a decidedly *civil* language, a language of our common citizenry. As one blogger put it so bluntly, referring to a famous story about the first Shi'i Imam Ali not being able to sleep because one of his soldiers had stolen an anklet off the feet of a Jewish girl, "they are

91

now tearing the pants off our young brothers and sisters and violently raping them, and you want us to think highly of Imam Ali having lost sleep about an anklet?"

These are indeed terrifying times that are trying our souls, a time when principles sacrosanct to who and what we are have become the first victims of a vicious banality that has no regard for the most basic human decency. The moral and political crisis of the Islamic Republic, however, is the emancipatory passage of both Islam and republicanism from a flawed and murderous mismatch. As political Zionism, militant Islamism (or Christian or Hindu fundamentalism for that matter) has been a horrific historical *faux pas*. Once Muslims are released from implicating their multifaceted religion in a singularly militant ideology or a tyrannical theocracy they are freed once again to embrace their faith and piety in the cosmopolitan worldliness of its historical experiences; and once Iranians are freed from force-feeding their democratic aspirations down the narrow throat of an "Islamic Republic," they have ipso facto joined a public space in which their societal modernity gives birth to enduring democratic institutions. None of this is either to call for or else to discourage the dismantling of the Islamic Republic altogether—a historical eventuality beyond any single person's wish or will. This is simply to begin to think through the current crisis of the Islamic Republic and the ungodly terror it has visited upon a nation for over 30 years, and articulate manners of civil liberties that will be needed to sustain enduring democratic institutions—during or after this Islamic Republic.

The difficult task ahead is that the barbarity of the violent custodians of the Islamic Republic is evidently determined to dictate the terms of not just obedience to it but in fact, and far more dangerously, the manner of opposition to it. It is not that by violence the belligerent leadership of the theocracy demand and exact obedience; it is that by the selfsame violence they are determining the terms of opposition to their illegitimate rule. The Green Movement as a result needs to be exceedingly conscious not to fall into that easy trap. At the writing of this passage, I cannot think of a more noble act of resistance to their barbarity than the peaceful, pious, and gracious gathering of the families of the unjustly incarcerated activists in Evin prison for their *Eftar* (breaking their fast) on the first day of Ramadan 1430/August 22nd, 2009—spreading their *Sofreh* and sporting their green plastic plates.

The central volume of the Green Movement is very conscious not to allow the violent behavior of the militarized security apparatus of the Islamic Republic to determine the course of their actions, thoughts and strategies. They insist on crossing over their psychological barrier and coming to terms with a future bereft of violence. There is in fact no better way of fighting against this regime than celebrating life, embracing joy—*ba del-e khonin lab khandan biyavar hamcho jam*, as the contemporary Persian poet Houshang Ebtehaj teaches us:

> With a heart full of blood
> Bring forth a pair of smiling lips—
> Just like a cup of wine.

This assessment is not a wish. It is written in the body of the movement. "I am absolutely convinced," writes Fatemeh Shams, a prominent blogger whose own husband Mohammadreza Jala'ipour was arrested and charged with plotting to topple the regime, "that the incarceration of people like Somayyeh Towhidlu, Hamzeh Ghalebi, Mohammadreza Jala'ipour, Sa'id Shari'ati, and Shahab al-Din Tabataba'i is to target a young generation that wishes both to have faith and is committed to reform, is both preoccupied with [the betterment of] our homeland and is committed to legal frameworks and societal principles. This time around, the fundamentalists have targeted a generation that was determined to follow a third path, the path upon which it was possible to be religious but not be retrograde, to be a reformist but oppose the toppling of the regime and violence."

Fatemeh Shams' appraisal of the movement, based on being born and raised in an Islamic Republic, is exceedingly important because there is always the danger that the moral dissolution of the regime and the systemic violence that it is perpetrating upon its own citizens might succeed in dictating the terms of opposition to its benighted rule. The transmutation of legitimate resistance to tyranny into tyrannous terms in the opposite direction is already very much evident among the Quixotic expatriate "opposition" that speaks, writes, and acts in precisely the same vulgar manner that their counterparts in the Islamic Republic do. Outside the purview of the Islamic Republic and the violent expatriate "opposition," it has generated against itself, the Green Movement needs to stay clear of both and turn to our extended literary humanism to sustain its moral rectitude. For all the terror that the Islamic Republic has perpetrated upon Islam and Muslims, the heart of Islam beats happily and resoundingly, sound and safe, where it has always been, in the best of our poetry, in our literature, in the solitude of our disbelief or belief. With one line of Sa'di we can rebuild our humanity, with one *ghazal* of Hafez we will learn how to love anew, and in the aromatic pages of Rumi we will look for God again—just before we turn to our sagacious Khayyam and play hide-and- seek with Him.

The Iranian *Baha'is* and the American Muslims[4]

In their latest communiqué regarding the fate of seven arrested members of the Baha'i religious minority in Iran, Amnesty International has expressed grave concern that they may in fact face the death penalty if they were to be found guilty of the charges of "espionage for Israel," "insulting religious sanctities," and "propaganda against the system."

As the Islamic Republic of Iran experiences the most serious challenge to its legitimacy in its 30-year history, the vulnerability of religious and ethnicized minorities is the most accurate barometer of the crisis that all Iranians face in these dire circumstances. Of all the various Iranian minorities, historically the weakest and most vulnerable has been the Baha'i community. As the world's attention is rightly drawn to the fate of prominent reformists charged with treason, and to the arbitrary arrest, torture, rape, and murder of young Iranians, the fate of the Iranian Baha'is should not be eclipsed under the cloud of other civil rights abuses, for they represent much more than their own small community.

All minorities have always been at the mercy of belligerent authorities, particularly when they face a crisis of legitimacy. Kurds in Western Iran, Arabic-speaking communities in the south, Azaris in the north, as well as the Turkmans and Baluchis in the west have been at the forefront of such discriminations, which has in turn instigated chronic separatist movements in these areas. At the same time, Iranian Zoroastrians, Jews, and Armenians have also faced varying degrees of discrimination, at official or cultural levels and registers, as they have joined their Muslim brothers and sisters in opposing domestic tyranny and foreign intervention alike.

Among all these minorities, the Baha'is remain the most fragile in part because of intra-Shi'i sectarian hostilities that go back to mid-nineteenth century and the rise of a vastly popular messianic movement known as Babism, of which the contemporary Baha'is are an offshoot, though its adherents believe themselves to be the followers of an entirely new religion—in fact the very last Iranian monotheistic faith with over 5 million followers scattered over 200 countries.

While other religious minorities are specifically protected under the Constitution of the Islamic Republic, this is not the case for the Baha'is. Article 13 of the constitution has specifically and exclusively recognized Zoroastrian, Jewish, and Christian Iranians as "the only recognized religious minorities, who, within the limits of the law, are free to perform their religious rights and ceremonies, and to act according to their own canon in matters of personal affairs and religious education." The word "only" in this article seems specifically designed to exclude the Baha'is from this clause as is Article 14 of the constitution that exempts from respecting the rights of the minorities of those "who refrain from engaging in conspiracy or activity against Islam and the Islamic Republic of Iran." The accidental location of the Baha'is holy sites in Haifa, Israel, which goes back to the late Ottoman period, obviously predates the establishment of the Jewish state in 1948, and over which the Baha'is have obviously had absolutely no control, been a principle source of harassment and intimidation against the Baha'is.

In the face of the systematic abuse of the Baha'is' civil liberties, there is very little that the American government can do, particularly in the aftermath of the Bush presidency and 8 years of widespread Islamophobia in the United States that did not leave even the last presidential campaign unscathed. Having waged war on two Muslim nation-states, the US government is not in a position to defend the rights of non-Muslim minorities in their own homeland. In addition, during the 8 years of Bush presidency, being a Muslim suddenly became a liability in the United States, creating PR problems even for President Obama's middle name. It was not until former Secretary of State Colin Powel came out strongly against such vilification of Muslims that a prominent public figure put the problem on national consciousness.

As much as the US government is not in a position to come to the Baha'is' aid, Muslim Americans are perfectly poised to voice their outrage against the abuse of religious minorities in Iran or anywhere else in the Muslim world, for they know what it feels to be a political pariah and a religious minority in an overwhelmingly alternate context. Since the terrifying events of 9/11, American Muslim communities have endured much religious and racial profiling and suspicion, as they have seen the terms and icons sacrosanct to their faith maligned and ridiculed from one end of Western Europe, up to North America and down to Australia. Multiply that experience manifold and extend it back to the late nineteenth century and that would be the experience of the Iranian Baha'is, trapped inside their own homeland, banned from confessing to or exercising the terms of their own sacrosanct principles. The experiences of Muslims as a minority here in the United States (or in Europe for that matter) gives them a unique position to raise their voice against the abuse of non-Muslim minorities in Iran and the rest of the Muslim world.

In a world now defined by the presence of multiple faiths inside many nation-states, and as American Muslims learn to come together to protect their own constitutional rights in an old democracy, it is only befitting if they were to raise their voice in defence of other religious minorities seeking to secure their basic rights to religious liberties in countries aspiring to become democracies. The fate of Iranian Baha'is is not only a matter of their fundamental civil rights in the context of any republic, Islamic or otherwise but is the very corner-stone of democratic citizenship without which the Muslim majority of Iranians is denied their constitutional protection. Watch the fate of the Iranian Baha'is carefully. The day they are free to practice their religion freely and without fear, Iranians at large have finally secured their civil liberties.

Notes

1. An earlier version of this essay was published in *al-Ahram* (August 13–19, 2009).
2. An earlier version of this essay was published as "Iran confronts rape, torture allegations" in CNN.com (August 22, 2009).
3. An earlier version of this essay was published as "The Crisis of an Islamic Republic" in *al-Ahram* (September 10–16, 2009).
4. An earlier version of this essay appeared on CNN.com (September 16, 2009).

5

Responses to the "Left" and Other Accounts of the Situation

Left is Wrong on Iran[1]

When a political groundswell like the Iranian presidential election of June 2009 and its aftermath, the excitement and drama of the moment expose not just our highest hopes but also our deepest fault lines, most troubling moral flaws, and the dangerous political precipice we face.

Over the decades I have learned not to expect much from what passes for "the Left" in North America and/or Western Europe when it comes to the politics of what their colonial ancestry has called us, "the Middle East." But I do expect much more when it comes to our own progressive intellectuals—Arabs, Muslims, South Asians, Africans, and Latin Americans. This is not a racialized bifurcation, but a regional typology along the colonial divide.

By and large this expectation is apt and more often than not met. The best case in point that I can offer is the comparison between what Azmi Bishara has offered about the recent uprising in Iran and what Žižek felt obligated to write. Whereas Bishara's piece (with aspects of which I have had reason to disagree) is predicated on a detailed awareness of the Iranian scene, accumulated over the last 30 years of the Islamic Republic and even before, Žižek's (with the conclusion of which I completely disagree) is entirely spontaneous and impressionistic, predicated on as much knowledge about Iran as I have about the mineral composition of planet Jupiter. The examples can be multiplied by many, when we add what Azmi Bishara has written to those by Mustafa El-Labbad and Galal Nassar, for example, and compare them to the confounded blindness of Paul Craig Roberts, Anthony DiMaggio, Michael Veiluva, James Petras, Jeremy R. Hammond, Eric Margolis, and many others. While people closest to the Iranian scene write from a position of critical intimacy, and with a healthy dose of disagreements, those farthest from it write with an almost unanimous exposure of their constitutional ignorance, not having the foggiest idea of what has happened in that country over the last 30 years, let alone the last 200 years, and then having the barefaced chutzpah to pontificate one thing or another—or worse take more than 70 million human beings as stooges of the CIA and puppets of the Saudis.

After the initial *faux pas* of the Left on Iran, a number of critical pieces have been published—among them Reese Erlich's fine essay, "Iran and Leftist Confusion" (*Common dreams*, June 29, 2009) and Saeed Rahnema's equally compelling criticism "The Tragedy of the Left's Discourse on Iran" (*Znet*, July 10, 2009)—in which the hurried leftist reflections have been taken rightly to task. Missing in these apt criticisms, however, has been the reasons behind the Left's suspicion and reticence in embracing the Iranian uprising.

For that reason, let me begin by stating categorically that in principle I share the fundamental political premise of the Left, its weariness of the US imperial machination, of major North American and Western European media (but by no means all of them) by and large missing the point on what is happening around the globe, or even worse seeing things from the vantage point of their governmental cues, which they scarcely take to task. It has been scarce a few months since we have come out of the nightmare of the Bush presidency or the combined chicaneries of Dick Cheney, Donald Rumsfeld, Paul Wolfowitz, and John Ashcroft, or of the continued calamities of the "war on terror." Iran is still under the threat of a military strike by the Jewish state, or at least more severe economic sanctions, similar to those that are responsible for the death of hundreds of thousands of Iraqis during the Clinton administration. Iraq and Afghanistan are burning, Gaza is in utter desolation, Northern Pakistan is in deep humanitarian crisis, and Israel is stealing more Palestinian lands every day. With all its promises and pomp and ceremonies, President Obama is yet to show in any significant and tangible way his change of course in the region form the previous administration.

So John Pilger and others have every legitimate reason to be suspicious of the collective euphoria about President Obama, as do many on the Left to be suspicious of any national scene in a vitally important geopolitics that may in fact tilt the balance of game on the side of the United States and its imperial projects and the expansionist belligerence of the Jewish state. The left is right to be deeply concerned about all this. The US congress, prompted by AIPAC, pro-war vigilantes lurking in the halls of power in Washington DC, and the Israeli warlords and their propaganda machinery in the United States are all excited about the events in Iran and are doing their damnedest to turn it to their advantage. Even the man who wanted to "bomb, bomb, bomb Iran," the former presidential candidate Senator John McCain, seems to sport a green bandana these days.

Having said that, however, the political stand of certain strident segments of the left on the current Iranian crisis is deeply disappointing and is a serious cause for concern about the moral courage, political insights, and normative health of our collective intelligence. Having principled positions on geopolitics is one thing, being blind and deaf to a massive social movement is something entirely different, as being impervious to the flagrant charlatanism of an upstart demagogue like Ahmadinejad. The sign and the task of a progressive and agile intelligence is to hold on to those principles and seek to incorporate a massive social uprising into its *modus operandi.*

My concern here is not with that retrograde strand in the North American or Western European left that is siding with Ahmadinejad and against the masses of millions of Iranians daring the draconian security apparatus of the Islamic Republic. They are a lost cause, and frankly no one could care less what they think of the world. What does concern me is when an Arab intellectual like As'ad AbuKhalil opts to go public with his assessment of this movement—and what he says so vertiginously smacks of recalcitrant fanaticism, steadfastly insisting on a belligerent ignorance.

On his Web site, "Angry Arab," As'ad AbuKhalil finally has categorically stated that he is "now more convinced than ever that the US and Western governments were far more involved in Iranian affairs during the demonstrations than was assumed by many." He then tries to be cautious and cover his back by stipulating, "let us make it clear: the United States, Western, and Saudi intervention in Iranian affairs does not necessarily implicate the Iranian protesters themselves. And even if some of them were involved in those conspiracies, I do believe that the majority of Iranian protesters were motivated by domestic issues and legitimate grievances against an oppressive government." This latter stipulation is in fact worse than that categorical statement about the conspiratorial plot behind the movement, for it seeks to play fancy speculative footwork to cover up a moral bankruptcy—that he dare not take a stand, one way or another. AbuKhalil's final edict: "I was just looking at US and Western media coverage of Honduras: where the situation is rather analogous and you cannot escape the conclusion that the US media were involved with the US government of a conspiracy the details of which will be revealed years from now." In other words, since the US media is not covering the Honduras development as closely as it does (so AbuKhalil fancies) the Iranian event, then the US media is in cahoots with the US government in fomenting unrest in Iran, and thus this movement is manufactured by the US imperial designs and the Saudi servile aid in the region, and though we may not have evidence of this yet, we will learn of its details 30 years from now, when a Stephen Kinzer comes and writes an account of the plot, as he did about the CIA-sponsored coup of 1953.

One simply must have dug oneself deeply and darkly, mummified inside a forgotten and hollowed grave on another planet not to have seen, heard, and felt for millions of human beings risking their lives bravely and precious liberties and pouring into the streets of their cities demanding their constitutional rights for peaceful protest. Thousands of them have been arrested and jailed, their loved ones worried sick about their whereabouts; hundreds of their leading public intellectuals, journalists, civil and women's rights activists rounded up and incarcerated, harassed, and even tortured, some being brought to national television to confess that they are spies for "the enemy." There are pregnant women among those leading reformists arrested, as are such leading intellectuals as Said Hajjarian who is paralyzed, having barely survived an assassination attempt by precisely those in the upper echelons of the Islamic Republic who have yet again put him and his wheelchair in jail. Three prominent reformists, all heroes of the Islamic Revolution—Khatami, Mousavi, and Karroubi—a former President, a former Prime Minister, and a former Speaker of the House to this very Islamic Republic—are leading the opposition, charging fraud, declaring Ahmadinejad's government illegitimate. The seniormost Grand Ayatollah of the land, the octogenarian Ayatollah Montazeri, has openly declared Khamenei's government illegitimate. The Iranian parliament is deeply divided and in turmoil. A massively militarized security apparatus has wreaked havoc on the civilian population—beating, clubbing, tear-gassing, and plain shooting at them. University dormitories have been savagely raided by plainclothes vigilantes and students beaten up with batons, clubs, kicks, and fists by oversized thugs.

Millions of Iranians around the globe have taken to the streets, their leading public figures—philosophers like Abdolkarim Soroush, clerics like Mohsen Kadivar, public intellectuals like Ata Mohajerani, filmmakers like Mohsen Makhmalbaf, pop singers like Shahin Najafi, footballers of the Iranian national team—countless poets, novelists, scholars, scientists, women's rights activists, *ad infinitum*—have come out and voiced their defiance of this barbarity perpetrated against their brothers and sisters.

Not a single sentence, not a single word, that I just uttered comes from CNN, the *New York Times*, Al Arabiya, or any other source that As'ad AbuKhalil loves to hate.

None of these means anything to Mr. As'ad AbuKhalil? Can he really face these millions of people, their best and brightest, the mothers of those who have been cold-bloodedly murdered, tortured, beaten brutally, paralyzed for life, and tell them they are stooges of CIA and the Saudis, and that CNN and Al Arabiya have put them up to it?

AbuKhalil has every legitimate reason to doubt the veracity of what he sees in the American media. But why does he watch CNN and al-Arabiya so much? Is there no reality beneath and behind their mis/representations? Suppose a massive tsunami happens in the Pacific Ocean, a major volcano erupts in Japan—if CNN and the *New York Times* report these, then there is something fishy about that tsunami or that volcano? At what point does a legitimate criticism of media representations degenerate into an illegitimate disregard for the reality itself—or has a sophomoric reading of postmodernity so completely corrupted our moral stand that there is no reality any more, just representation?

As'ad AbuKhalil dismisses a massive social uprising that is unfolding right in front of his eyes as manufactured by Americans and the Saudis, trapped as he is inside a cocoon where evidently he watches nothing but CNN, with an occasional contact with a certain "Dale" fellow who recommends a book to him that is about half a century late telling Iranians what they have known long before As'ad AbuKhalil and this comrade "Dale" were even born.

What else does AbuKhalil know about Iran, except for what he has learned from CNN, Al Arabiya, or Dale? Anything? Thirty years (predicated on 200 years) of thinking, writing, mobilizing, political and artistic revolts, theological and philosophical debates—any of it rings any bell for Professor AbuKhalil? Do the names Mahmoud Shabestari, Abdolkarim Soroush, Mohsen Kadivar, among scores of others, mean anything to him? Has he ever listened to these young Iranians speak, cared to learn the lyrics of their music, watched the films they make, gone to a photography exhibition they have put together, seen any of their art work, or perhaps glanced at their myriads of newspapers, journals, magazines, Weblogs or Web sites? Are all these stooges of America, manipulated by CIA agents, bought and paid for by the Saudis? What depth of intellectual depravation is this?

As'ad AbuKhalil is happy with himself picking up a fight with the "Western media" for not reporting a staged demonstration protesting the murder of Marwa al-Sherbini, but seems to be utterly ignorant of the fact that members of the Iranian parliament are taking Ahmadinejad's government to task for the hypocrisy of shedding crocodile tears for the murdered Egyptian women, while completely dumb when it comes to the massacre of Muslims in China, as they were when Muslims were being murdered in Chechnya, for fear of offending their handful of allies in the world.

In his most recent posting, our "Angry Arab," as As'ad AbuKhalil calls himself on his blog, has this to say about Iran: "For the most reliable coverage of the Iran story, I strongly recommend the *New York Times*. I mean, they have Michael Slackman in Cairo and Nazila Fathi in Toronto, and they have "independent observers" in Tehran. What else do you want? If you want more, the station of King Fahd's brother-in-law (Al-Arabiya) has a correspondent in Dubai to cover Iran. And according to a report which just aired, Mousavi received 91% of the vote in "an elite neighborhood." I kid you not. They just said that. What about Iranians themselves? They have no reporters, no journalists, no analysts, no pollsters, no economists, no sociologists, no political scientist, no newspaper editorials, no magazines, no blogs, no Web sites? If As'ad AbuKhalil has this bizarre obsession with the American or Saudi media that he loves to hate, does that psychological fixation *ipso facto* deprive an entire nation of their defiance against tyranny, their agency in changing their own destiny?

What a terrible state of mind to be in! AbuKhalil has so utterly lost hope in us—us Arabs, Iranians, Muslims, South Asians, Africans, Latin Americans—that it does not even occur to him that maybe, just maybe, if we take our votes seriously the United States and Israel may not have anything to do with it. He fancies himself opposing the United States and Israel. But he has such a deeply colonized mind that he thinks nothing of us—of our will to fight imperial intervention, colonial occupation of our homelands, *and* domestic tyranny at one and the same time. Because he believes that if we do it then the Americans and the Saudis must have put us up to it. He is so utterly lost in his own moral desolation and intellectual despair that in his estimation only Americans can instigate a mass revolt of the sort that has unfolded in front of his eyes. What an utterly frightful state for an intellectual to be in—no hope, no trust, no courage, no imagination, no hope. That we as a people and as a nation, collectively, have fought for over 200 years for our constitutional rights has never occurred to As'ad AbuKhalil. What gives a man the authority to speak so cavalierly about another nation—about which he knows nothing.

Ten years I spent watching every single Palestinian film I could lay my hands on before I opened my mouth and uttered a word about Palestinian cinema. I visited every conceivable archive in North America and Western Europe, travelled from Morocco to Syria, drove from one end of Palestine to another, was blessed by the dignity of Palestinians resisting the indignity of a criminal occupation of their homeland, walked and showed bootlegged videos on mismatched equipments and stolen electricity from one Palestinian refugee camp in Lebanon to another, then I went to Syria and found a Palestinian archivists who knew infinitely more about Palestinian cinema than I did, and I sat at his feet and learned humility—and I still did not dare put pen to paper or open my mouth about anything Palestinian without asking a Palestinian scholar—from Edward Said to Rashid Khalidi to Joseph Massad—to read what I had written before I dared to publish it. This I did not do out of any vacuous belief in scholarship but out of an abiding respect for the dignity of Palestinians fighting for their liberties and their stolen homeland—fearful of the burden of responsibility that writing about a nation's struggles puts on those of us who have a voice and an audience.

For people like Žižek social upheavals in what they call the Third World is a matter of theoretical entertainment. It is an old tradition that goes back all the way to Sartre on Algeria and Cuba in the 1950s, down to Foucault on Iran in the 1970s. That does not bother me a bit. In fact I find it quite entertaining—watching grown people make complete fool of themselves talking about something about which they have no blasted clue. But when someone like As'ad AbuKhalil indulges in cliché- ridden Leftism of the most banal variety, it speaks of a culture of intellectual laziness and moral bankruptcy so outrageously at odds with the struggles of people from which we emerge. Our people are not to conform to our tired, old, and cliché-ridden theories. We need to bypass armchair critics and catch up with our people . Millions of people, young and old, lower and middle class, men

103

and woman, have poured in their masses of millions into the streets, launched their *Intifada*, demanding their constitutional rights and civil liberties. Who are these people? What language do they speak, what songs do they sing, what slogans do they chant, to what music do they sing and dance, what sacrifices have they made, what dungeons have they crowded, what epic poetry are they citing, what philosophers, theologians, jurists, poets, novelists, singers, song writers, musicians, Webloggers soar in their soul, and for what ideals have their hearts and minds ached for generations and centuries? A colonized mind is a colonized mind whether it is occupied by the European Right or by the cliché-ridden Left: It is an occupied territory, devoid of detail, devoid of substance, devoid of love, and devoid of a caring intellect. It smells of aging mothballs, and it is nauseating.

Looking for the Middle Class in all the Wrong Places[2]

In his astute take on the current electoral crisis in Iran ("An alternative reading," *al-Ahram*, June 25 to July 1, 2009), by far the best in the literature so far, Azmi Bishara lays out a very concise premise for our reading of the unfolding event but, alas, reaches a hasty and flawed conclusion. What I respectfully submit below is in a spirit of utter solidarity with the leading Palestinian intellectual whom I admire as a guiding light in our critical assessment of where we stand in our contemporary world.

Having carefully outlined the totalitarian disposition of the Islamic Republic, Azmi Bishara proceeds to identify two ways in which it differs from other totalitarian regimes: (1) that it has a democratic component that allows for two opposing camps to compete for elected offices, not in fact too dissimilar in their political formations to the Republican and Democratic parties in the United States; and (2) that it is in fact a religion that constitutes the state ideology and not an alien or imported ideology shared by the political elite but alien to the rest of society.

Compared to China and the Soviet Union, Azmi Bishara rightly concludes, "looking at Iran from the perspective of its degree of democratic competition, tolerance of criticism and peaceful rotation of authority in accordance with set rules, it is much closer to the pluralistic democracies in the West than to a dictatorial regime." Be that as it may, he is equally aware of the fact that indeed a totalitarian ideology permeates all spheres of private and public life, not unlike the power of consumer ideologies doing pretty much the same in North American and Western European societies.

All these accurate and insightful observations, however, begin to move on more icy grounds when Azmi Bishara observes that "the criticisms levelled at the regime on the part of a broad swath of youth who have joined the reformists, especially those from middle class backgrounds who are more in contact with the rest of the world, are reminiscent of the grievances aired by the young in Eastern Europe, who held that their regimes deprived them of their individual and personal freedoms, the freedom to choose their way of life and the Western consumer lifestyle."

This careless use of the key term "middle class" soon coagulates into a more solid assertion that is even more seriously flawed: "While not dismissing or belittling such criticism," Azmi Bishara observes, "it is important to bear in mind that these people are not the majority of young people but rather the majority of young people from a particular class [i.e., middle class] ... Most of the youth from the poor sectors of society support Ahmadinejad."

From this false premise, Azmi Bishara then proceeds to assert that "the mood among those who think that their votes carry more weight qualitatively than the numerically greater votes of the poor, and who may actually believe that they represent the majority because they form the majority in their own parts of town even if they are the minority in the country, has an arrogant, classist edge."

The assumption that supporters of Mousavi and/or Karroubi, or indeed that masses of millions of people who have poured into the streets of Tehran and other cities, come from "the middle class" is a common fallacy that Azmi Bishara shares with quite a number of others who are watching the Iranian scene from a theoretical distance that conceals more than it reveals. Even a seasoned historian of contemporary Iran like Ervand Abrahamian, a distinguished professor of history in New York, has come out with a similar assessment, though with more qualified phrases. "The core of the support for Mousavi," Abrahamian has told Amira Haas of the *Haaretz*, "is in fact university graduates and educated people, who can be described as middle class, and who are a clear product of the welfare state and the policy of expanding social services in force since the establishment of the [Islamic] Republic. Ahmadinejad's support base is whom I call 'evangelical' rather than 'fundamentalist.' These are not the poor, but the religious poor - between 20 and 25 percent." Abrahamian's latter point about what he calls the "evangelical poor" has a number of other serious holes in it, which for now I will leave out.

The problem with the false impression about this mysterious "middle class" is not only that it distorts the reality of what we are observing in Iranian cities, but that it also inadvertently fuels the conspiratorial theories among certain segments of the North American and Western European Left that take this observation one delusional step further and believe that CIA (on behalf of Neoliberal economics) is behind this "velvet revolution." That particular pathology needs a separate diagnosis—but the false premise of a "middle class" support for Mousavi, particularly by people I deeply admire, needs more urgent attention.

Of a total Iranian population of 72 million, upward of 70% are under the age of 30. While the total rate of unemployment under Ahmadinejad, predicated on correspondingly high numbers under Khatami's two-term presidency, is 30%, this rate, according to Djavad Salehi-Isfahani, the most reliable Iranian economist around, for the young people between the ages of 15 and 29 (some 35% of the total population) is 70%. So seven out of every ten people in this age cohort can scarce find a job, let alone marry, let alone have children and form a family—and in exactly what phantasmagoric definition of "the middle class" can they hope to be included?

Let me give another statistic. You must have noticed the overwhelming presence of women in these demonstrations. Right? Now: 63% of university entrants in Iran are women, but they make up only 12.3% of the workforce. In other words, one out of every two women university graduates earn their degrees and then go back to live with their parents, remain a burden on their limited budget, and can only hope to leave their parents' home if they can find a husband among those 3 out of 10 young men who may be lucky enough to find a job that would enable them to marry. In what Marxist, Keynesian, or Neoliberal definition of this blessed "middle class" would they fit—exactly?

Now, consider another fact. If we were to believe the official tabulation of the presidential election, which I have no way of proving otherwise (though that they are rigged is now a "social fact"), twice as many of these young voters have voted for Ahmadinejad as they did for Mir-Hossein Mousavi, Mehdi Karroubi, and Mohsen Reza'i put together. In other words, the official results shoot the argument of pro-Mousavi "middle class" in the foot—for we will end up either with the bizarre proposition that pro-Mousavi Iranians voted for Ahmadinejad, if the results are accurate, or else the perfectly plausible possibility that the unemployed and thus by definition the poor voted for Mousavi, if the results are rigged. Either way, the supporters of Mousavi are not the upper middle class bourgeoisie who think their votes are worth more than others.

But all these and similar statistics pale in comparison to another statistic that shows the real horror at the heart of the Islamic Republic— for which not just Ahmadinejad but in fact the entire militant disposition of the ruling elite is responsible. In 1997, some 3 million high school graduates participated in the Iranian national university entrance examination, of which only 240,000 managed to pass through the Seven Tasks of Rostam and enter a university—namely the full capacity of the entire Iranian university system is less than 10% of the total applicants. So what happened to that more-than-90%? Where did they go—what job, what opportunity, what education?

The answer is frightful. A significant portion of this remaining 90% is absorbed into various layers of militarized security apparatus, including the *Basij* and the *Pasdaran*. If in fact anyone qualified for that dreaded "middle class" status it is precisely this component of the 15–29 year olds who have not made it to the university system and have joined the security apparatus of the regime—for they have a steady job (of clubbing people on the head, or else shooting to kill them point blank, if they do not behave), can marry, form a family, and have a solid investment in the status quo and be considered "middle class." In other words, instead of spending the national budget on expanding the university system, and then generating jobs, the custodians of the Islamic Republic, not just Ahmadinejad, insecure of their own legitimacy as they are, rather spend it on fortifying a security apparatus that keeps their aging banality in power.

Now: Of course Ahmadinejad is not entirely responsible for this sad state of affairs. Iranian economy is 85% oil-based, and an oil-based economy is not labor intensive, and the Iranian "middle class" has always, since the nineteenth century, been a feeble and shaky proposition. But Azmi Bishara's assumption that "Ahmadinejad is less a representative of Iranian conservatives than a rebel against them from within their own establishment," or that "he has lashed out against them, including corrupt clergy, using the principles of the Islamic Revolution as his weapons" is deeply flawed. Of course there were corruption in the two previous administrations of both Khatami and Rafsanjani that preceded him and gave free reign to neoliberal privatization and its catastrophic consequences. But in what particular

107

way has Ahmadinejad corrected that course? The course was not corrected in any way. The battle between Ahmadinejad and Rafsanjani is not a battle between revolutionary purity and aging corruption. It is a battle between a retiring elite and an emerging, previously lower ranking echelon that is coming up for grabs. It is a romanticism of the most dangerous sort to imagine Ahmadinejad as a man who "wants to restore the revolution to its youthful vigor and gleam." He is so patently transparent that all you have to do is sit through ten minutes of his charlatanism during the televised presidential debates to see through the rampant lumpenism with which he operates. The only way that "he distributes oil revenues among the poor" is by recruiting them into the multi-layered and brutal security apparatus of the *Basij* and the *Pasdaran*. This, again, is not his invention. He simply carries on an innate insecurity of the regime by over-investing in security forces.

Azmi Bishara is far more on an accurate course when he rightly observes that "Ahmadinejad's populist rhetoric has come as a boon to racist Western policies toward the Arabs, Muslims, and easterners in general. The certificate of exoneration he has handed Europe for the Holocaust is catastrophic in every sense." And yet again he overrides his own insight by suggesting, "Ahmadinejad has also shocked the West with a set of correct principles that challenge the colonialist legacy and that are rarely uttered now that everyone has been tamed to the axioms of Western racist arrogance." How so? How could a banal and parochial reiteration of certain truisms about colonialism and imperialism qualify Ahmadinejad for "correct principles?" Just because the Arab and Muslim world is cluttered with gutless collaborationists in positions of power it does not mean that an irresponsible demagogue qualifies for courage or "correct principles." Quite to the contrary: Ahmadinejad's imbecilic speech in Geneva in the course of Durban II in April 2009 was chiefly responsible for whitewashing the Israeli massacre of Palestinians in Gaza in December 2008 to January 2009.

The cause of Palestinian national liberation has to be rescued from such demagoguery and rewritten into our democratic aspirations in an emerging geopolitics of which these young Iranians, men and women, lower and middle class, demonstrating in the streets of their cities are in its vanguard. Democratic institutions and civil liberties ought to be equally salvaged and rescued from the combined banality of Neoliberal economic and Neoconservative chicanery. Israel loves nothing more than its own mirror image in the region—fanatical regimes that make it feel at home in the neighborhood, and would thus much rather deal with corrupt collaborationists from one end of the Arab and Muslim world to another, punctuated by populist demagogues.

This is a moment in our history that requires visionary leadership. Consider the case of Hassan Nasrallah. After his initially wise and judicious position, refusing to take side, he rushed to congratulate Ahmadinejad for his "victory." This was a terrible strategic mistake. He must have known for a fact that the solidarity of Iranians with the noble causes of Palestine and Lebanon is not contingent on Ahmadinejad's victory or defeat. His subsequent move that "Iran is under the authority of the *Wali al Faqih* and will pass through this crisis," was of course far more astute but too little too late, coming after Ali Khamenei had authorized the bloody crackdown of the uprising. Why could Nasrallah not show the same judicious poise when the Hezbollah lost the Lebanese parliamentary election to the 14 March coalition of Saad Hariri? What is the difference between the cause of democracy in Lebanon and in Iran? But lest my criticism of Nasrallah is abused by people in Tel Avi and Washington DC, let me make sure that they know that we are more than capable of tolerating the principle of democratic dissent, even in the direst circumstances, without losing sight of what racist colonial settlement is the single most dangerous threat to democracy in our region.

We must learn from those who are risking their lives in the streets of Iran and muster courage and imagination to face and read it proactively, rather than collapse back to a structural-functional analysis of the *status quo* in which we are in effect saying to ourselves, "Listen folks, we are Orientals. Oriental despotism is written into our DNA, and charlatans like Ahmadinejad are the best we can produce"—as our false guilt mistakes their lumpenism for their proletarian origins and projects, and then allows for our intellectual reticence to theorize their victory as self-evident. We need, for the sake of our posterity, to think better of ourselves.

Adjusting Our Lenses[3]

In a short essay that Abbas Amanat, a scholar of the nineteenth century Iran at Yale University, was asked to write for the *New York Times* on the current crisis in Iran, he asserts that what we are witnessing is "the rise of a new middle class whose demands stand in contrast to the radicalism of the incumbent President Ahmadinejad and the core conservative values of the clerical elite, which no doubt has the backing of a religiously conservative sector of the population." He further adds, "the new middle class wants to participate in the discourse of democracy and create its own indigenous secularism ... It is sensitive to Iran's image abroad and does not wish to be portrayed as extremist and uncouth."

This learned position of a leading scholar very much sums up the common wisdom that Iranian expatriate academics are offering to an excited public mesmerized by the massive demonstrations they witness on their television sets or computer screens and are eager to have someone make sense of them. In part because of these hurried interpretations, the movement that is unfolding in front of our eyes is seen as basically a middle class uprising against a retrograde theocracy that is banking on backward, conservative, and uneducated masses who do not know any better. While these illiterate and "uncouth" masses provide the populist basis of Ahmadinejad, the middle class is demanding a neoliberal economics and an open market civil society. Highly educated, pro-western, and progressive Iranians are thus placed on the Mousavi's side, while backward villagers and the urban poor are on Ahmadinejad's. The fact that in North America and Western Europe usually unveiled and fluent English-speaking women are brought to speak on behalf of the women demonstrators further intensifies the impression that if women are veiled or do not speak English fluently then they must be Ahmadinejad supporters.

This is a deeply false dichotomy that projects a flawed picture to the outside world and is predicated on the spin that a very limited pool of expatriate academics are putting on a movement that is quite extraordinary in Iranian political culture and is yet to be unpacked and its full dimensions assayed with patience, open-mindedness, and above all a categorical abandoning of old clichés that conceal more than they reveal what we are witnessing.

The fact is that given the structural limitations of a nascent democracy that is being crushed and buried in Iran under a Shi'i juridical citadel, opposition to Ahmadinejad is fractured into the followers of three candidates with deeply divided economic programs and political positions. Mr. Mousavi is universally known as a hardcore socialist in his economic platform and a social reformist in his politics. Mehdi Karroubi is far more to Mousavi's Right in his economic Neoliberalism and social conservatism. Mehdi Reza'i, meanwhile, is even more to the Right of Karroubi in his social conservatism but to his Left in his economic platform.

What above all challenges the reading of this event as a middle class revolt against "uncouth radicalism" is a crucial statistics that Professor Djavad Salehi-Isfahani, one of the most reliable Iranian economists in the United States, provides in the very same set of responses that *New York Times* has solicited from these experts. "Young people ages 15–29," Mr. Salehi reports, "make up 35 percent of the population but account for 70 percent of the unemployed." The overwhelming majority of the people pouring into streets of Tehran and other major cities in support of Mr. Mousavi are precisely these 15–29 year olds. How could then this be a Middle Class uprising if the overwhelming majority of those who are supporting it and putting their lives on the line are in fact jobless 15–29 year olds who still live with their parents—who cannot even afford to rent an apartment, let alone marry and raise a family and join the middle class in a principally oil-based economy?

Another crucial statistic that Mr. Salehi does not cite is the fact that 63% plus of university entrants in Iran are women, but only 12% are part of the labor force. That means that the remaining 51% are out of jobs, and yet the most visible aspect of these anti-Ahmadinejad demonstrations is that women visibly outnumber men. How could jobless men and women be participating in a massive middle class uprising against their "uncouth" leaders?

If we were to look closely at Mousavi's campaign commercials, various iterations of his social and economic platforms since he entered the race, and the presidential debates with all the other candidates, we see that a sizable component of his supporters are indeed university students, young faculty, and the urban intellectual elite—such as filmmakers, artists, and the literati. But the fact is that a major constituency of Mousavi is also the urban poor and particularly the war veterans who have no respect for Ahmadinejad's inglorious war records but full of unsurpassed love and admiration for Mousavi because of his role as a fiercely dedicated prime minister during the Iran–Iraq War (1980–1988). Conversely, there is a significant segment of the traditional middle class, the *bazaaris*, that is in fact the beneficiaries of Ahmadinejad's economic policies of governmentally subsidized commodities and services and thus supports him.

As for the "uncouth" among the Iranian peasantry, Eric Hoagland, a senior scholar of Iran with decades of experience in rural areas, has recently said when he hears reports that Ahmadinejad's support base

111

is rural, he is left quite baffled. "Is it possible that rural Iran," he asks pointedly, "where less than 35 percent of the country's population lives, provided Ahmadinejad the 63 percent of the vote he claims to have won? That would contradict my own research in Iran's villages over the past 30 years, including just recently."

A similar iteration of the couth versus the uncouth is evident in the piece that Professor Janet Afary, a historian, has written in the same issue of the *New York Times*, and in which she concentrates on Mr. Mousavi's wife, Ms. Zahra Rahnavard, as a case of the "sexual politics in Iran." "Ms. Rahnavard," Professor Afary reports, "was a leftist long before she became an Islamist." The two are not of course mutually exclusive in Iranian context, but the more important point in this dichotomy is what Professor Afary actually leaves out in this short piece but is far more clear in her book on *Sexual Politics in Modern Iran* (2009) where, relying on the German social psychologist Erich Fromm, she interprets Ms. Rahnavard's turn from Secularism to Islamism in the psychopathological terms of "moral aloneness," and a turn to religion as "absurd and degrading."

The fact is that we really do not know how this uprising is going to pan out, and yet we seem to be in too much of a rush to assimilate it backward to inherited assumptions that may have in fact lost their validity in face of this new reality. I am convinced that we are witness to something quite extraordinary, perhaps even a social revolution that is overriding its economic foregrounding. Although there are many similarities, this is a very different event from the 1977–1979 Islamic Revolution. I am not sure that this movement either sees itself as a revolution or will actually transmute into one. Given the brutality it faces, it has no choice but opt for a nonviolent civil disobedience route. The age of ideological warfare is over in Iran. If anything, this momentum is the closest event in Iran to the Civil Rights Movement of the 1960s in the United States, and precisely like that its economic foregrounding is couched in social demands. We need to adjust our lenses and languages in order to see better, and there is no better adjustment than just cautiously, hopefully, and responsibly watch what is being unfolded in front of us and read it accordingly. This movement is ahead of our inherited politics, floating ideologies, or mismatched theories. We need to sit back, hope for the best, and let this inspirational movement of a whole new generation of hope teach us courage and humility.

The Discrete Charm of European Intellectuals[4]

One morning, as Gregor Samsa was waking up from anxious dreams,
he discovered that in his bed he had been changed into a monstrous
verminous bug.

Kafka, The Metamorphosis (1915)

The idea of Žižek waking up one morning from anxious dreams and discovering that in his bed he had been metamorphosed into a Shiite Muslim and catapulted into the rambunctious capital of an Islamic Republic is quite wickedly intriguing. Whoever put him up to that idea? "What's happened to me," he would wonder like the good old Gregor Samsa, as his bewildered gaze would turn to the window and notice the dreary weather—the raindrops falling audibly down on the meta window ledge in Evin Prison in Tehran, making him quite melancholic for his comfortable apartment in his native Ljubljana.

I can well imagine Žižek in those prison pajamas, sitting next to an array of Iranian reformists, wishing he were only there in name and spirit, like Max Weber, Jürgen Habermas, or even Richard Rorty. But here he was, in person, in Tehran, jailed and charged with having plotted a velvet revolution to topple the Islamic Republic. With your permission though I will only imagine Prof. Žižek in Evin Prison and not in Kahrizak, for given what the custodians of the Islamic Republic have been doing to their inmates in that particular detention center, it would be quite disconcerting, if not outright disrespectful, to imagine the leading European intellectual under those circumstances.

After Michel Foucault terribly misread the Iranian Revolution of 1979, wrote a few quite curious articles for *Corriere della Sera* and kept his admirers and detractors busy and confounded for over some 30 odd years, we have had no prominent European philosopher collecting his courage, mustering his wits, and crossing that proverbial psychological barrier, enough to say something sensible about those Muslim Orientals the way Žižek did recently about the postelectoral violence in Tehran. This was a good thing to have happened under the circumstances when American neoliberals and neoconservatives had joined forces, patting Iranians on the back for their knowledge of Nabokov and Habermas alike—all in the condescending and custodial tone of "now, ain't that cute, they are reading *Lolita* and *Legitimation Crisis* in Tehran." In no uncertain terms, bless his soul, and at a time when what in North America and Western Europe passes for "the

113

Left" was quite baffled as to how to respond to the mid-June uprising in Iran, Žižek came out and brushed them all aside and defended our cause, all in a clear and confident prose. We—we the native sons and daughters, as Richard Wright would say about us colored folks from Chicago's South Side to Iran's southern provinces—were quite happy to welcome the dandy, groovy, and cool philosopher in our midst.

This was no "orange" revolution Georgia style, Žižek told Europeans; nor was it a neoliberal-democratic secular uprising. He countered those who thought "Ahmadinejad really won: [that] he is the voice of the majority, while the support of Mousavi comes from the middle classes and their gilded youth." He dismissed those "who dismiss Mousavi as a member of the cleric establishment with merely cosmetic differences from Ahmadinejad." and above all he denounced "the saddest of them all [who] are the Leftist supporters of Ahmadinejad: what is really at stake for them is Iranian independence. Ahmadinejad won because he stood up for the country's independence, exposed elite corruption and used oil wealth to boost the incomes of the poor majority—this is, so we are told, the true Ahmadinejad beneath the Western media image of a Holocaust-denying fanatic." He missed a couple of crucial characters who also championed Ahmadinejad's cause—failed academics and career opportunists who seized upon their chance to cash in on the beleaguered "President's" need for someone with half decent English to rush to CNN to defend his cause, or else deeply alienated second generation Iranians growing up in suburban North America and rushing to Tehran and Isfahan to discover their roots in Ahmadinejad's deep pocket and take a stance against "Western decadence" and its "liberal democracy." It was and it remains quite a pathetic scene. But we thought Žižek was quite eloquent in sorting things out and setting the record straight.

We all read all those wise, timely, and true words and admired the big old funny philosopher and thought he deserved all those accolades coming his way, including a whole International Journal of Žižek Studies, no less, and dubbed "the Elvis of Philosophy." How could he be so smart and know all these things! Europe may not be literally the creation of the Third World after all, as Fanon suspected, and "Western civilization" does indeed sound like a good idea, as Gandhi conjectured.

The analytic becomes a bit blearier, however, when Žižek comes to his own assessment of what's happening in Iran. "The green colors adopted by the Mousavi supporters and the cries of 'Allahu akbar!'

that resonated from the roofs of Tehran in the evening darkness," he surmised, "suggested that the protesters saw themselves as returning to the roots of the 1979 Khomeini revolution, and canceling out the corruption that followed it." What happened, how, and by what authority? How did Žižek make that conclusion? Just from the color green? Wow! That is some serious *Farbenlehre*! How can we, mere mortals, make that transcontinental assumption, that 30 years after the Islamized revolution of 1977–1979, this new generation wishes to go back and relive that experience—and saying so on the basis of two floating signifier of a color (green) and a chant (*Allahu Akbar*)? No, sir! It makes no sense. So the question is: who was the native informer who thus misinformed the European philosopher? For that is precisely how Foucault was mishandled by his handlers when he was chaperoned to Tehran in 1979—some Islamist activists got hold of him and kept feeding him food to theorize.

Žižek provides more evidence: "This was evident in the way the crowds behaved: the emphatic unity of the people, their creative self-organization and improvised forms of protest, the unique mixture of spontaneity and discipline. Picture the march: thousands of men and women demonstrating in complete silence. This was a genuine popular uprising on the part of the deceived partisans of the Khomeini revolution."

This is all partially apt and impartially accurate. But how does it amount to these demonstrators wishing to go back 30 years ago and no longer being "the deceived partisans of the Khomeini revolution"? Logic? It does not add up. What we were witnessing was a genuine, grassroots, social uprising (in part spontaneous, in part *the logical growth* and in fact the forbidden fruits of a crescendo of events that began 30 years ago and thus by definition cannot be a going back to 30 years)—but whence and how the assumption of a retrograde, nostalgic return to the fetal position of the nascent revolution? Shouldn't in fact "the improvised forms of protest" (a very apt description) alert the philosopher that we have had, perhaps, a massive generational shift, an epistemic shift even (occasioned by the narrative exhaustion of ideological legacies, exacerbated by the internet, computer literacy, and cyberspace social networking) after which there is no illegal/illogical U-Turn?

I am, to be sure, completely on the same page with Žižek when he rightly says, "We should contrast the events in Iran with the US intervention in Iraq: an assertion of popular will on the one hand, a foreign imposition of democracy on the other"; or when he asserts, "the events in Iran can also be read as a comment on the platitudes of Obama's Cairo speech, which focused on the dialogue between religions: no, we do not need a dialogue between religions (or civilizations), we need a bond of political solidarity between those who struggle for justice in Muslim countries and those who participate in the same struggle elsewhere." I so wish Žižek had written Obama's Cairo speech, instead of Rahm Emanuel (or whoever else helped him write it). But none of this provides evidence that those who were demonstrating were after reliving their parents' lives 30 years ago.

No, sir! If anything, they were (all the indications suggested that they were) sick and tired of that revolutionary zeal and political animus and were in fact holding their parents responsible for the calamity they had found themselves in, hanging over their heads the banality of the idea of an Islamic Republic, or, even worse, a *Velayat-e Faqih*. So still the mystery persists—how in the world did Žižek conclude that these masses of demonstrators were seeking a return to 30 years? The man is a philosopher, must have studied logic—so where is the 2+2 that equals this particular 4?

I am also (almost entirely) with Žižek when he rightly says that "Ahmadinejad is not the hero of the Islamist poor, but a corrupt Islamo-fascist populist, a kind of Iranian Berlusconi whose mixture of clownish posturing and ruthless power politics is causing unease even among the ayatollahs," though I wish he had reconsidered that "Islamofascist" bit—for it exposes his Eastern European angst of out-Western Euro-peanizing Western European anxieties more than it reveals anything about Iran. Iran is not fascism, though fascism has always threatened Iran. Islam is an abstraction, as much capable or abhorrent of fascism as Judaism and Christianity—and I have not heard of any talk about "Judeofascism" 60 years after the Zionist armed robbery of Palestine, or "Hindufascism," for that matter, after any of the Hindu slaughters of Muslims in India. Be that as it may, Žižek has me on his side when he says, "His [Ahmadinejad's] demagogic distribution of crumbs to the poor shouldn't deceive us: he has the backing not only of the organs of police repression and a very Westernized PR apparatus. He is also supported by a powerful new class of Iranians who have become rich thanks to the regime's corruption—the Revolutionary Guard is not a working-class militia, but a mega-corporation, the most powerful centre of wealth in the country."

Chapeau—as some Francophone Lebanese say on such occasions! But, yet again that nagging "but," the assumption that if you are poor you are gullible and for Ahmadinejad, or you do not see through his incompetence and chicaneries, that you have no dream, no democratic aspiration for your homeland, is positively disconcerting to come from an otherwise progressive European philosopher. I know of quite a number of rich second generation Iranians, grown up in suburban north America, who are totally taken by the darvishi demeanor and lumpenism of the demagogue infinitely more than any poor person from southern Tehran would. But, hey, what can you do—but move on!

Žižek, again, loses me completely when he declares that we have to draw a clear distinction between the two main candidates opposed to Ahmadinejad, Mehdi Karroubi, and Mousavi. Karroubi is, effectively, a reformist, a proponent of an Iranian version of identity politics, promising favors to particular groups of every kind. Mousavi is something entirely different: he stands for the resuscitation of the popular dream that sustained the Khomeini revolution ... Now is the time to remember the effervescence that followed the revolution, the explosion of political and social creativity, organizational experiments and debates among students and ordinary people. That this explosion had to be stifled demonstrates that the revolution was an authentic political event, an opening that unleashed altogether new forces of social transformation: a moment in which "everything seemed possible." What followed was a gradual closing-down of possibilities as the Islamic establishment took political control. To put it in Freudian terms, today's protest movement is the "return of the repressed" of the Khomeini revolution (Žižek, 2009 Web site).

"Closing down of possibilities" might be a fine euphemistic way of saying how Khomeini & Co. brutally suppressed alternative voices that wanted to have a say in the aftermath of the revolution—but the revolution itself, what occasioned these possibilities, was no meteor coming at Iran from the heavens. It was in the making for some 200 years— and it was poly-vocal from the outset. Khomeini aborted a full delivery of a healthy and robust republic and delivered a mismatched Siamese twin called "Islamic Republic," topped by an authoritarian doctrine called *Velayat-e Faqih*. What is happening today in Iran, as a result, is the full-bodied, material, symbolic, discursive, and institutional historicity of the multifaceted Iranian cosmopolitanism (that just remembering it makes you cringe with anger against these neo-liberal Americans who think they have discovered an earth-shattering phenomenon that Iranians read Habermas! finally bursting out of the tight and unbecoming medieval jurisprudence that was violently clothed around it.

Unless we begin where we must begin, upstream from the violent over-Islamization of the 1979 revolution in the course of the American Hostage Crisis of 1979–1980 and the Iran–Iraq War of 1980–1988, a fact that Žižek's precursor, Foucault, terribly failed to see, we are bound to fall into Žižek's trap of cyclical historiography, which in our case amounts to a vicious circle, spinning after our own tail, chasing after yet another charismatic father-figure we want to follow to kill by way of our version of what Freud called "deferred obedience," which in our case is actually "deferred defiance." That cyclical historiography also prevents you from seeing the nature of *leadership* in this movement and misleads you to come up with flawed assessments of people like Mousavi, Karroubi, or Khatami. Both Karroubi and Mousavi, and before them Khatami, are the *product* of this movement, and not this movement the product of their visions and leadership. If we begin with any kind of typological contradistinction between Karroubi and Mousavi in reading this movement, we will end up on a goose chase, or worse (better metaphor) yet, chasing like a puppy after its own tail, trying to figure out this movement. This movement invented a Mousavi, crafted a Karroubi, and envisioned a Khatami out of its deepest visions for a different future, which means killing its future father-figures at the very beginning by splitting them into at least three alternates and thus celebrating its own boastful bastardy — once and for all for Sohrab to outwit Rostam and set his mother Tahmineh and the rest of us free.

Let us not get too carried away with Persian mythology, lest we lose the European philosopher, and return to his familiar turf and simply suggest that instead of a Freudian "return of the repressed" in this particular case, we are better off with a Jungian "collective unconscious."

There is something about the Green Movement that prompts Žižek toward the Freudian "return of the repressed," except it is not repressed, for what we have is a perfectly alert and conscious attempt at the retrieval of the violently denied cosmopolitan political culture of a people that was militantly "repressed" (not in the Freudian psychoanalytic sense but in the Khomeinian political terms of sending club-wielding thugs to close down your newspaper and beating up your editorial staff so you would shut up and be quiet and not utter a word against the violent over-Islamization of a multifaceted revolution).

But Žižek's preference for Mousavi over Karroubi, and the way he talks about him, gives me a nagging suspicion that his native informer must have been a pro-Mousavi activist who set the European philosopher off on the same wrong track that Foucault was by his overzealous Islamist activists. Now, as someone who actually voted for Mousavi, I have nothing against that particular presidential candidate, but not to the point of collapsing the analytic of the phenomenon we are now facing into yet another cult of personality, to which we orientals (so we seem to our European orientalists) are particularly prone.

It is upon this Freudian slip, as it were, that Žižek then falls down like that very cat he invokes early in his essay, and just like that cat, he does not immediately notice it: "What all this means is that there is a genuinely liberatory potential in Islam: we don't have to go back to the tenth century to find a 'good' Islam, we have it right here, in front of us." Here, Žižek in fact picks up precisely where Foucault left off—concurring with the militant over Islamization of a worldly and polyvocal political culture, and then seeing an emancipatory force emanating from it. While Foucault saw this as the very "soul" of a soulless world that Marx had prophesied, and Žižek sees it as a warning to "the West" that unless they see Ahmadinejad for the charlatan that he is, Berlusconi and even worse is what is in the offing for his fellow-Europeans. The result, yet again, is all the same: Iran, Islam, as the rest of the world, is just a laboratory for testing the maladies that are threatening "the West." One might even trace this particular proclivity back to Max Weber himself, who begins his diagnosis of capitalist modernity with a reading of the Protestant ethics and "Western nationalism," and ends up in an Iron Cage that can only be broken down by chronic charismatic outburst. Fortunately for him, Weber was not alive to see Hitler and the Holocaust coming his particular German/European way, though he (and even before him Tocqueville) certainly saw them coming.

In the European context, and in the aftermath of the horrors of the Holocaust, at least Adorno and Horkhheimer saw to it that the dangerous instrumentalization of reason, written into the dialectics of the Enlightenment was fully exposed for Europe. But the same old nostalgia for charismatic outbursts (and thus Žižek's jaw-dropping "[but] Mousavi is something entirely different") seems to have transmuted into European philosophical fascination with bearded or bespectacled third world revolutionary prophets—at the heavy cost (for us) of helping distort our cosmopolitan worldliness, to which our religions are certainly integral but by no means definitive.

119

The problem with the European Left is that they care a little bit about just about everything, and yet there is nothing in particular about which they care deeply. This is very similar my old teacher Philip Rieff used to call "the Monroe Doctrine"—not the famous President James Monroe doctrine of warning Europeans to keep their hands off the Americas, but the little known Marilyn Monroe doctrine, named after the famous actress for having once said, "I believe in everything," and then pausing for a moment before saucily adding, "a little bit." The difference between European and colonial intellectuals is summed up in the difference between Sartre and Fanon, or between Foucault and Said. Sartre and Foucault cared widely about the entirety of the colonial and colonizing world, while Fanon and Said cared deeply about Algeria and Palestine, and from these two sites of contestation they extrapolated their politics and ethics of responsibility toward the rest of the world. Žižek is precisely in the same tradition and trajectory as those of Sartre and Foucault—caring widely but not deeply enough, for (and here is the philosophical foregrounding of their political proclivity for vacuous abstractions) they know widely and variedly but never deeply and particularly.

What passes for the Left in the United States is even worse. Since they have seen me (as one example among many) preoccupied with Iran, they think I have compromised my stand vis-à-vis American imperialism or its Israeli colonial outpost—for they too care in abstraction and act in generalities. I am preoccupied with Iran in 2009 precisely in the same way I have been with Iraq since 2003, and with Afghanistan since 2001 (when the best of these Americans thought Afghanistan was a "just war"), and precisely the same way I have been with Palestine all my adult life: from the site of specific crimes against humanity opens up your frame to see the rest of the world.

There is something charming about the European intellectuals when bored with nothing happening in Europe and turning their theorizing gaze beyond the banks of the Danube River. That antiquarian charm hangs over the memory of the Europe of our youth when we colored folks sought to sustain the hope with which we have been born and bred. Kafka concludes his *Metamorphosis* with a happy ending to Gregor Samsa's demise, when Mr and Mrs Samsa notice how much their young daughter Grete has grown up and become a "good looking, shapely" girl. Thinking to themselves that "the time was now at hand to seek out a good honest man for her. And it was something of a confirmation of their new dreams and good intentions when at the end of their journey their daughter stood up first and stretched her young body." The same is with the tall and handsome body of Žižek's fine essay on Iran, an indication that the European philosopher is finally ready to get up and move and wed his sharp intelligence to a singular cause, stop the promiscuous philandering with generalities and learn the honesty of a monogamous commitment to one moral site. Who was it who said, "O Plato! I can see horse, but not horseness!" Bless his soul! There used to be something worldly and exciting about European indulgence in generalities they call "philosophy," which now seems only so irresistibly charming the way one might feel about an old armchair sitting idly by at a marché folklorique in an old European town off the shores of LacLeman. Yea—I do sometimes miss them! No—come to think of it I wish never to see Professor Žižek in any of those unseemly prison pajamas at Evin in Tehran. It would be so unbecoming of our old Oriental ways to put a prominent philosopher on display like that. Let us wait for a few years—hopefully this Green Movement will become a *vanishing mediator*, and we will all be able to give him a warm welcome at Tehran University.

Reference

Žižek, S. "Berlusconi in Tehran." *London Review of Books* 31 (No. 14) (July 23, 2009): 3–7. Available at: http://www.lrb.co.uk/v31/n14/slavoj-zizek/berlusconi-in-tehran

Notes

1. An earlier version of this essay was published in *al-Ahram Weekly* (July 16–22, 2009).
2. An earlier version of this essay was published as "Looking in the wrong places" in *al-Ahram Weekly* (July 2–8, 2009).
3. An earlier version of this essay was published as "Iran conflict isn't class warfare" in CNN.com (June 22, 2009).
4. An earlier version of this article was published in *International Journal of Žižek Studies*, volume 3 (4)—Special issue: Žižek and Iran.

6

US Politics, Iran, and the Green Movement

Thirty Years Ago and Counting[1]

November 4th, 2009 is the 30th anniversary of the American Hostage Crisis, a turning point in Iranian history, the geopolitics of the region, and the US–Iran relations that have remained troubled ever since.

I am one of the last Iranian students who peacefully walked into the United States embassy in Tehran in July 1976 with a recently acquired Iranian passport and an even-more recently obtained acceptance letter from the University of Pennsylvania, a I-20 form as we used to call it then, and applied for a visa, received one, and boarded a plane and flew from Tehran to Philadelphia, and thus began my American sojourn when I was just over 25 years old. In just about a second and half (the way time flies these days), I will turn 60, and I will have a claim over Philadelphia and New York as my successive hometowns more than I do over the cities in which I was born and received my college education, Ahvaz and Tehran. In the course of a single lifetime, I have seen the demise and debacle of two homelands I have failed to see in friendlier terms.

Over the last month, and in anticipation of this symbolic day, an open-ended war has been waged between the supporters of the status quo and the champions of a groundswell in Iranian political culture. As Ahmadinejad's government and its clerical supporters are gearing up for business as usual of "Death to America!" chants and marches, the nonviolent, grassroots, civil rights movement has produced its own posters and placards, leading with the chant: "Death to No one!"

If Americans are cursed with a very short memory, Iranians have been plagued with a prehistorical longevity to their recollections. They talk about the Arab/Muslim conquest of the mid-seventh century AD, as if it happened the day before yesterday, for yesterday was when the CIA-engineered coup of 1953 happened. But this year around, commemoration of historical events has turned into a battleground for a happier and healthier future, rather than a tiresome marking of the troublesome past.

Iran and the United States have charted two divergent and hostile paths over the last 30 years. The legitimate fear of a US-led coup on the model of 1953 resulted in an illegitimate breach of diplomatic immunity and the taking over of the US embassy and its staff on November 4th, 1979. Ayatollah Khomeini then abused that crisis to build the institutional foundation of a theocracy, crack down on all alternative claims on that revolution, and when the American hostages had served their purposes, released them in January 1981, for by then he had bigger fish to fry in the course of Iran–Iraq War (1980–1988), under which smoke screen (which he prolonged long after Saddam Hossein had realized his folly and was ready for peace talks) he cracked down even more violently on internal opposition.

On the American side, the story was no less sad and catastrophic. Under President Reagan and subsequent US administrations, Saddam Hossein was armed to the teeth to invade and curtail the Islamic Republic, while at the same time the Afghan Mujahideen (soon to be transmuted into "the Taliban") were even more massively armed (via Pakistani intelligence and Saudi money—fueled by militant Wahabism) to battle the Soviets and prevent the spread of the Shi'i-inspired Iranian Revolution into Central Asia. The strategy succeeded, the Islamic Revolution turned inward, killed its own children, and aggressively degenerated into a terrorizing theocracy.

But soon the two monsters that the United States and its allies had created, Saddam Hossein and the Taliban, came back to haunt their creators. Saddam Hossein invaded and occupied Kuwait soon after the end of Iran–Iraq War, almost at the same time that Osama bin Laden and his al-Qaeda operation, feeding on the Talibanization of Afghanistan began a series of terrorist attacks on US interests that ultimately culminated in the events of 9/11, and then resulted in the US-led invasion of Afghanistan in October 2001 and of Iraq in March 2003. And our world has remained in the grips of that spiral of violence ever since.

Roger Cohen has just written a column for the *New York Times*, speculating what would have happened if the massive June demonstrations would have been successful in dismantling the Islamic Republic. If such Monday morning quarter-backing are not to be an academic exercise in futility, one must also wonder what would have happened if the coup of 1953 had not implanted a national trauma in Iran, so that the Grand Ayatollah had not abused its memory to eliminate alternative visions of Iran and consolidate a theocracy, and thus a multifaceted and cosmopolitan social uprising had succeeded to unfold its centuries-old-dreams of democratic institutions and civil liberties.

When on November 4th, you see throngs of young Iranians chanting "Death to No one!" they are not just challenging the brutal theocracy that is distorting their history and abusing their youth—they are also raising a gentle accusatory finger at their own parental generation.

Katie Couric's Sarah Palin Moment[2]

One of the most memorable episodes of the US presidential election of 2008 was the much-publicized September 2008 interview that CBS Evening News Anchor Katie Couric did with the then Alaska Governor and Republican vice presidential candidate Sarah Palin. Quite a number of embarrassing revelations dawned on the American presidential election scene after that interview, including the fact that the person potentially a proverbial heartbeat away from the US presidency could not name a single newspaper or magazine that she regularly read.

The interview turned out to be so crucial a piece in the course of that presidential election that garnered for Katie Couric the much coveted Walter Cronkite Award for Excellence in Television Political Journalism, with the judges considering that interview a "defining moment in the 2008 presidential campaign."

As fate would have it exactly a year after that fateful interview, Katie Couric was destined to have an equally, if not more, embarrassing Sarah Palin moment of her own.

In the course of a much anticipated interview with the belligerent Iranian president Mahmoud Ahmadinejad in late September 2009, Katie Couric raised the all-important murder of Neda Aqa Soltan in the course of postelection violence in Iran, which Ahmadinejad habitually dismissed as an unfortunate event in the course of a chaos that had been instigated by the United States and the United Kingdom.

Faced with Katie Couric's follow-up-question, and obviously performing a well-rehearsed move, Ahmadinejad then produced a picture, showed it to Katie Couric and asked her point blank: "Do you know [the woman in] this picture?" Katie Couric looked at that picture for a second and said "No." Ahmadinejad knew at that moment that he had his interlocutor where he wanted and drove the point even further and repeated his question, now producing a second picture, "Do you know this woman?" Katie Couric again said, now twice in a row, "No." After which Ahmadinejad immediately went for the kill, "Well, you can't be blamed for not knowing her," for, Ahmadinejad interjected, American politicians did not want her to know about that woman, while Neda Aqa Soltan had been turned into a *cause célèbre* by way of instigating public opinion against the Islamic Republic. Neda Aqa Soltan was killed in the course of a riot in Iran, he concluded, but the woman in those pictures was murdered in a German court of law. How come she did not know about that woman, while grilling him on Neda Aqa Soltan? He scored a point not just against a leading American journalist, but against reason, sanity, and decency .

There are more holes in Ahmadinejad's point than in that proverbial Swiss cheese, none of which occurred to Katie Couric, including the fact that the woman in that picture, Marwa Ali El-Sherbini, was the victim of a singularly vicious act of a Pro-Nazi racist, while Aqa Soltan was one among many other victims of rape, torture, and murder, systemic and endemic to the security apparatus of the Islamic Republic. But something more than Katie Couric's preparedness, presence of mind, and habitual journalistic tenacity were amiss in that interview.

Mr. Ahmadinejad might have rhetorically felt quite generous in forgiving Katie Couric for not knowing who Marwa Ali El-Sherbini was, just to make his point more forceful, but we might pause for a moment and ask why is it that she did not know who she was and how she was murdered. Hopefully the answer is not because she has a scarf in that picture and Katie Couric cannot tell one scarved woman from another. A more plausible question to ask is precisely the one she put to Sarah Palin: "Not to belabor the point ... I was curious what newspapers and magazines did you regularly read before you were tapped for this to stay informed and to understand the world ...?"

The case cannot be dismissed as one of a uninformed journalist ill-prepared for an interview with a master of diversionary tactics, for the fact is that Katie Couric is a superbly competent, courageous, and spontaneously tenacious journalist. So the question is what happened to all those fine qualities, on perfect display when interviewing Sarah Palin, in the interview with Ahmadinejad?

The tragic case of Marwa Ali El-Sherbini has been in the news all over the world not the least in the United States, and of course

126

throughout the Arab and Muslim world, and even, or particularly, in Europe. The Iranian state-controlled media, in particular, has been abusing the case of Marwa Ali El-Sherbini ever since Neda Aqa Soltan was killed, and the world began to pay attention to her murder to show "the hypocrisy of the western media"—and behold a star of "the Western media," sitting on the seat that once Walter Cronkite sat, having just won the prestigious prize set in his honor, a perfect case in point.

The answer to the puzzle of Katie Couric's Sarah Palin moment is neither in any conspiracy of the "Western media" to cover up the case of Marwa Ali El-Sherbini nor indeed can it be attributed to the incompetence of an inexperienced journalist unprepared for an important interview. The answer is in an endemic provincialism that still very much defines American journalism. This provincialism, to be sure, does not dwell in any absence of knowledge or care about the non-American scenes, but in an archival incarceration of that awareness in a part of the brain that seems to be incommunicado with the rest of a journalist's spontaneous competence. A fundamental analytic split parts the domestic and foreign issues that they simply do not connect, and unless and until they do, in a shrunken world no longer divisible into any domesticity or foreignness, we would not see that world more clearly.

Katie Couric interviewed Sarah Palin with a perfectly pitched combination of natural curiosity, disarming charm, and velvet tenacity. She went to interview Ahmadinejad with a robotic clumsiness of a rookie reporter with no commanding control over her material evidence. This rather typical predicament of American journalists habitually swings between two opposite poles: either yielding to become the inadvertent tools of propaganda for politicians they do not know well, or else, turning into exceedingly rude and abrasive interlocutors, making abusive psychopaths like Ahmadinejad look like the innocent victims of arrogance and disrespect. Katie Couric's collapse into the first of these two maladies has an enduring lesson for the professional journalist of the next generation. For personifying that lesson, Katie Couric deserves no less praise than she received after her interview with Sarah Palin.

A Tale of Two Cities[3]

On Wednesday, July 22, 2009, the United States House of Representatives Foreign Affairs Committee had a special hearing in Washington DC on "US Policy Toward Iran." Ten days later, on Saturday, August 1, 2009, scores of leading Iranian reformists, the most courageous public intellectuals and civil servants the country has produced over the last 30 years, were put on a grotesque mockery of a trial, charged with treason and conspiracy to topple the Islamic Republic via what the Prosecution termed a "velvet coup." These two events have produced two crucial documents, one the official transcript of the hearing in the House Foreign Affairs Committee in Washington DC, transcribed in mostly conversational English, and the other the official indictment of the Public Prosecutor in Tehran, delivered in clerically inflected Persian.

The peripheral presence of one person in both these documents points to a central concern in the Iranian civil rights movement that commenced in the aftermath of the June 2009 presidential election. When Abbas Milani, an Iran analyst employed at the Hoover Institution in California, appeared in front of the congressional hearing, chaired by House Foreign Affairs Committee Chairman Howard Berman, the attendees must have had no clue that his name and reputation would soon appear in the official indictment half-way around the globe in the Islamic Republic of Iran; and when ten days later, exactly that happened and the very same Abbas Milani was mentioned by name in the official indictment of the Public Prosecutor in Tehran; even the conspiratorial hallucinations of the prosecution could not have fathomed that the selfsame Abbas Milani had just about ten days earlier appeared in the US congress, elbow to elbow with the most notorious neocon artists this land has produced, effectively plotting the various scenarios of toppling the Islamic Republic.

Soon after his name appeared in the indictment, Abbas Milani rushed to put his own spin on it in *The New Republic* (the journal that brought you Azar Nafisi), making fun of the poor English of the officials of the Islamic Republic, and light of his role in the opposition, suggesting how falsely he is accused. In this piece, Milani said nothing about his appearance at the House Foreign Affairs Committee, just about ten days before his name popped up in Iran.

Washington DC (July 22, 2009)

"Mr. Chairman, Ladies and Gentlemen," thus Abbas Milani began his testimony in front of the House Foreign Affairs Committee on July 22, 2009, "Let me begin by thanking the Chairman and the Ranking member of the Minority for affording me a chance to speak to your august gathering. The last time I talked here, Congressman Lantos held the gavel and he embodied in his life and vision the best of America as the 'city on the hill.' I am humbled by his memory."

After the sycophantic solemnity of that opening, Milani proceeded to report to the committee, according to the official transcript of the hearing, that the Islamic Republic was in deep trouble, that "no more than twenty percent of the seventy million population of Iran ... can be said to support the status quo," and that Khamenei's "days as the infallible spiritual leader have mercifully ended." Milani then assured the members of the committee that "the regime has aggressively pursued a nuclear policy that seems unmistakably bent on developing at least the technological capability of making and delivering a nuclear bomb."

Milani then places himself between two binaries he offers as flawed approaches to Iran, policies that have not served the American interests best. The first flawed approach was by the "regime apologists, sometimes appearing in the guise of scholars and experts, as well as a few companies eager to do business in Iran. [they] have claimed the regime invulnerable and resolute, and the democratic forces at best dormant and bereft of resolve." These people have argued, Milani reports, that "the business of American policy is business ... and as the regime is here to stay, the US must make a 'grand bargain' with it expeditiously. Forfeit any attempt at regime change, offer the regime all security guarantees its paranoid vision demands, and in return expect that the regime will keep a promise it will make not to develop the bomb."

On the other side of these "regime apologists" stand "the second flawed policy [which] was offered by those who exaggerated the weaknesses of the regime. Using understandable concerns of citizens in Israel and the West about a nuclear Iran, they advocated a policy of 'regime change'." In Abbas Milani's estimation, in between these two flawed approaches stood what he termed "smart diplomacy and smart sanctions that curtail and contain the regime's ability to engage in mischief around the world while sending a positive message of support to the democratic forces of Iran. This policy must have as its ultimate goal the idea of helping Iran become a democratic polity."

Milani warns against a military strike on Iran, not because it kills people, or that it plunges the United States into yet another murderous quagmire next to Afghanistan and Iraq, but because it "saves the day for Khamenei and his cohorts and is sure to lead to the regime's open

129

and aggressive search for the bomb." He further believes, "based on all we know from Iranian history and human psychology, a military attack on Iran will invariably force the now disgruntled Iranians to rally around the flag, and eschew opposition to the regime." So military strike is politically counterproductive to the American goal of regime change. Abbas Milani has better, smarter ideas.

After his prepared remarks, Abbas Milani engages in a very collegial conversation with the members of the House Foreign Affairs Committee and his co-panelists, three of whom Patrick Clawson of the Washington Institute for Near East Policy, Orde Kittrie of the Foundation for Defense of Democracies, and Michael Rubin of the American Enterprise Institute advocate the imposition of more severe economic sanctions on Iran; while Suzanne Maloney of the Brookings Institution and Karim Sadjadpour of the Carnegie Endowment for International Peace were more reticent and thought the Congress should wait until "the dust has settled" over the current crisis before imposing sanctions. Abbas Milani chimes in quickly though and insists that the United States and its allies should impose "multilateral and crippling sanctions" on Iranians and not merely "half-baked" sanctions. They are no good.

The objective of the sanctions, the hearing concurs, is not just to prevent Iran from acquiring the Bomb, but also help what they term "the opposition," and it is right here that Karim Sadjadpour reports to the committee that "many members of the opposition and the population actually are starting to come around. Their views toward sanctions have changed ... They're starting to see value in it." Milani agrees with Sadjadpour that indeed "the opposition" and even the "population" at large wishes for a "multilateral and crippling sanctions" imposed by the United States and its allies on them.

From here the meeting gets more focused and purposeful, for now it becomes clear that these "multilateral and crippling sanctions" ought to be part of a larger scheme, when we hear Rep. Dan Burton (R-IN) comparing Iran to Nazi Germany, by way of advocating harsher sanctions, or when he adds that if sanctions did not work, Iranians "need to know what's coming next." Rep. Dana Rohrabacher (R-CA) clarified what was "coming next" when she told the panel, "we can do more than just sanctions," meaning covert operations in support for the opposition "so that they will have the material well-being ... to take on that government themselves." From there, Rep. John Boozman (R-AR) proceeded to argue that he will support Israeli bombing of Iran, while Orde Kittrie proposed that it would be better for the United States to carry out any military action because "we have the right capacity."

Abbas Milani's idea of imposing multilateral and crippling sanctions was thus integrated into covert operations and military strikes, by Israel and/or the United States, in order to prevent the Islamic Republic to get its hand on the bomb, while "helping the opposition."

Tehran (August 1, 2009)

In about 10 days after Abbas Milani's testimony in the US congress, the public trial of the leading reformists commenced in Tehran on August 1, and a curious aspect of the official indictment of the public prosecutor is the number of times that this very Abbas Milani's name appears as a key factor in charging the accused with sentiments, thoughts, and activities designed to overthrow the regime. The prosecution builds a case against the defendants by connecting them to Abbas Milani.

The indictment of the Tehran Prosecutor General begins with quoting from the Yunus/Jonas Chapter of the Qur'an (X: 21) "And when We make people taste of mercy after an affliction touches them, lo! they devise plans against Our communication. Say: Allah is quicker to plan; surely Our messengers write down what you plan." The expression "they devise plans/*Idha lahum makrun*" is a clear reference to those whom the Prosecutor General believes had been plotting to overthrow the government.

The indictment then proceeds to praise the heroism of the Iranian people for participating in their massive millions in the election. This was a sign of true religious democracy/*mardomsalari dini*. But alas, the indictment regretfully interjects, the enemies of the Islamic Republic want to disrupt and abuse this victory. It then quotes the Leader, Ayatollah Khomeini, for ridiculing an "American Zionist millionaire," meaning George Soros, who had boasted that he spent 10 million dollars and toppled the regime in Georgia. It then goes into theoretical details of the difference between a "velvet coup" and a "military coup." Gene Sharpe, a leading American theorist of nonviolent struggle, is then mentioned by name as the principal analyst of velvet coups: "*mobarezeh ye 'ari az khoshunat/*aka velvet coup." Velvet coups are slow in motion, the indictment stipulates, nonviolent, and civil, and before you know it they have toppled the regime. The Open Society Institute, the Rockefeller and Ford foundations, as well as the

131

Freedom House and the Council for Foreign Relations are part of this American set up, the indictment self-assuredly asserts.

The rest of the indictment quotes "a spy who is currently in custody and for security reasons we cannot name him." This spy has given the prosecutor more details of this velvet coup and confessed that he too is part of the plot. In Israel the spy has met with the Middle East Media Research Institute (MEMRI), in Europe he knows of the activities of Radio Free Europe, among other operations, while in the United States he is familiar with the Berkman Center for Internet and Society, directed by John Palfrey, who has told the Iranian Spy, the indictment says, that he is in fact a grandson of Kermit Roosevelt, the CIA contact point who was in charge of the 1953 coup. This model of velvet coup has been perfected in Poland, Georgia, Serbia, and Croatia. For Iran, the spy has reported to the prosecutor, the United States has opted for the model of "election" as a ruse eventually to topple the regime and reinstate a secular government in its stead.

The velvet coup has a triumvirate, so says the indictment: intelligence, media, and execution. The most significant of organizations in charge of such velvet coups is the Hoover Institution, which has an "Iran Democracy Project," and it is right here that Abbas Milani figures prominently.

"Abbas Milani," the indictment reports, "was arrested during the Shah's time because of his leftist activities. Later he converted into a die-hard monarchist. After the revolution he lived in Iran for a few years, but then he left Iran for the United States, where he has written many books in which he has praised the achievements of the Pahlavi regime. He eventually became a leader of the opposition, with a marked difference with other members because of his connections to the reformists." The spy has also informed the Prosecutor General that Abbas Milani's "Iran Democracy Project" is interested in Iranian folklore, music, Weblog, and sexuality. He is also in direct contact with the leading reformists, some of them on trial, and others having left the country. "For CIA," the indictment concludes, "Abbas Milani is more important than Reza Pahlavi because Milani is well-connected to the reformists."

The indictment proceeds with further details, weaving an account that basically amounts to the argument that there has been a well-connected, well-financed, long in duration, conspiracy against the Islamic Republic by "the West," and those on trial have been its knowing and willing agents inside Iran, and as such they ought to be prosecuted for treason and brought to justice.

Between the US Congress and an Islamic Kangaroo Court

These two documents represent two enduring ailments with the world—an imperial arrogance that presumes anything that happens anywhere around the globe is its business, on one side, and the hallucinatory psychosis of an Islamic Republic that thinks the whole world is conspiring against it, on the other. In Washington DC, a congressional hearing brings together people with a very thin and dubious claim on knowing anything about a country half way around the globe (thinking that by including two native informers among them they have given the hearing an air of authenticity), and with in fact a decidedly arrogant and hostile intent to malign it, with the single purpose of seeing how best to dismantle its government—with crippling sanctions, covert operations, or military strikes. In Tehran, the best and most dedicated public intellectuals and civil servants of the country are paraded and humiliated on national television in a kangaroo court in order to discredit a grassroots uprising for civil liberties. Having been at times kidnapped off the streets, illegally incarcerated, at times tortured or otherwise forced to confess to ridiculous charges, with their families and friends enduring unimaginable suffering, these defendants are planted inside a phantasmagoric plot to overthrow the regime. In between these two complementary pathologies, the fragile flowering of a civil rights movement is at stake and stands to suffer or survive. The Hoover Institution here represents a crucial case when the name and reputation of a right-wing American think-tank, part of what Lewis Lapham has called a "Republican propaganda mill," is abused to discredit a grassroots, inborn, and massive civil rights movement.

The official indictment of the Prosecutor General in the kangaroo court of the Islamic Republic is a historic document detailing the psychotic paranoia of a regime obsessively conscious of its own illegitimacy, and blaming the whole world for its own troubles. To be sure, the Islamic Republic is not the only illegitimate operation prone to such paranoia. A systematically organized, omnipotent, and omnipresent "enemy" that acts as the principal trope of this indictment is identical in its vacuity and persistence with the selfsame "enemy" that kept appearing in George W. Bush's "war on terror" statements. "The enemy is wounded," he used to say in the catastrophic aftermath of the US-led invasions of Afghanistan and Iraq, "but the enemy is still capable of global operations ... we will not relent until the organized, international terror networks are exposed and broken and their leaders held to account for their acts of murder." The belligerent constitution of a fictive "enemy" is where all fascistic politics thrives. "The pinnacle of great politics," wrote famously the Nazi political theorist Karl Schmitt in *The Concept of the Political* (1927), "is the moment in which the enemy comes into view in concrete clarity as the enemy." This obsessive fixation with an amorphous enemy is also precisely the mindset of the beleaguered custodians of the Islamic Republic.

The hallucinatory delusions of the Islamic Republic notwithstanding, Abbas Milani does indeed work for the Hoover Institution, and he does indeed co-direct an "Iran Democracy Project." The Hoover Institution, not in the estimation of that indictment but in fact as diagnosed by such leading American critical thinkers as Lewis Lapham is a hotbed of neoconservative machination, of treacherous, imperial, militaristic, interventionist thinking (part of what in his "Tentacles of Rage" [2004] Lapham calls "the Republican Propaganda Mill")—and that is precisely where Abbas Milani's services are brewed in the neighborhood of such notorious infamies as Dinesh D'Souza, the author of *What's so Great about America* (2002), and Stanly Kurtz, the author of "Democratic Imperialism" (2003), in whose company must also be squarely placed Abbas Milani's "Can Iran Become a Democracy?" (2003). The question that remains valid, quite independent of any abuse of it by the illegitimate apparatus of the Islamic Republic, is what exactly is he doing in California directing a democracy project for Iran—from which vantage point he is then invited to advise the US congress on manners of dealing with Iran that include crippling sanctions, covert operations, and military strikes.

What these facts, even before they are transmuted into the propaganda machinery of the Islamic Republic, entail are the imperial arrogance of sitting in California or Washington DC and deciding matters of life and death for millions of human beings half way around the globe. What Milani terms "smart diplomacy" for him amounts to "multilateral crippling sanctions"—and for others in his company mixed with covert operations and military strikes. Without being either multilateral or crippling, the sanctions that President Clinton imposed on Iraq before President Bush took office was partially responsible for the death of hundreds of thousands of Iraqi children, which is perhaps nothing compared to that 14 million that according to his own estimation stand between Abbas Milani and his "Iran

Democracy Project" to move from the sunny coasts of California to the sandy shores of the Persian Gulf.

What is particularly alarming about this congressional hearing is the identical terms with which it paves the way toward a repetition of the Iraq scenario, though in this case Abbas Milani is presenting himself as a creative combination of what Fouad Ajami, Kanan Makiya, Ahmad Chalabi, and Zalmay Khalilzad did together for Iraq. The problem for Abbas Milani, however, is that the ruling banality in Tehran are made of precisely the same cloth as he is, and they have caught him in his game and upped the ante on him—and the nascent Iranian civil rights movement is caught between his machinations in the United States and the charlatanism of his kindred soul Mahmoud Ahmadinejad in the Islamic Republic.

The presence of Abbas Milani in both these documents marks the identical parasitical forces that seek to distort and destroy a grassroots democratic movement in Iran, which is launched against both foreign intervention and domestic tyranny. In Washington DC, Abbas Milani helps the US congress contemplate and plot economic sanctions, covert operations, and even military strikes in order "to help" the democratic movement in Iran, while in Tehran, the Iranian counterparts of the same sort of people who had gathered in that congressional hearing were weaving together a phantasmagoric tale of foreign intervention, velvet coups, and "cultural NATO," as they term it, in order to discredit that very movement. In Washington DC, Abbas Milani and his co-panelists seem entirely ignorant of the fact that their very gathering, ipso facto, was in complete denial of—and in fact criminally damaging to—that grassroots Green Movement; while in Tehran, a mere suggestion of that Washington hearing was enough to use and abuse it to discredit even more the movement. While on the surface the Washington meeting was in opposition to the court in Tehran—they are both in fact completely identical in their militant disregard for a people and their democratic aspirations.

The moral of the story is neither to underline the undaunted proclivity of an incompetent empire to meddle in other people's affairs nor to expose the militant paranoia of an Islamic Republic completely conscious of its illegitimacy and unconscious of its propensity to hallucinatory magic realism in weaving bizarre stories together (from Jürgen Habermas to George Soros plotting to topple the Islamic Republic); nor indeed is it to mark a rather unremarkable career opportunism of a comprador intellectual. Like all hallucinations, the

135

stories that the Spy and the Prosecutor have told each other in this indictment distort and abuse reality to their own advantage, and like all other native informers, Abbas Milani is after spinning his tale in a manner that sustains his frequent flyer program to Washington DC. Forget about the political paranoia of the Prosecutor General and take the account of Abbas Milani's "Iran Democracy Project: at Hoover institution and his machination with the neocon artists in the US congress to your own critical judgment and ask yourselves what will the end result of a hearing that speaks of crippling sanctions, covert operations, and military strikes sound like to an already jittery and criminally suspicious regime.

In between those two distortions and above the careerism of one native mis-informer, however, runs—now quietly and now thunderously—the beautiful river of a massive democratic movement that will not be stopped until it reaches its destination. Iranians are enduring ungodly violence these days, targeted against their body and soul by those presumably in charge of protecting them. The noblest and most courageous amongst them—men and women, young and old, clericals and lay—have paid heavily with their lives and liberty. Their fate will be decided neither behind closed hearings in Washington DC, nor in kangaroo courts in Tehran. The battlefields of their history are now the streets and alleys of their own indomitable spirit.

The Flawed Logic of a Congressional Hearing[4]

In a recent congressional hearing, House Foreign Affairs Committee Chairman Howard Berman called the Iran Refined Petroleum Sanctions Act "a sword of Damocles over the Iranians" that will soon come down if President Obama's diplomatic overture did not show signs of success by the fall. That sword is no mere metaphor and might kill more than the President's diplomatic overture.

Of the six invited panelists to this hearing, three—Patrick Clawson of the Washington Institute for Near East Policy, Orde Kittrie of the Foundation for Defense of Democracies, and Michael Rubin of the American Enterprise Institute—insisted that the United States should impose more severe economic sanctions on Iran; while Suzanne Maloney of the Brookings Institution and Karim Sadjadpour of the Carnegie Endowment for International Peace were counseling that Congress should wait until "the dust has settled" over the current crisis before imposing such sanctions. Abbas Milani of the Hoover Institution, however, upped the ante and insisted that the United

States should impose "crippling sanctions" and not merely "half-baked" measures.

The spirit of the meeting could not have been lost on any of the participants when Rep. Dan Burton (R-IN) compared Iran to Nazi Germany, thus advocating new and harsher sanctions, or when he added that if sanctions did not work, Iranians "need to know what's coming next." As to what exactly was to come next, Rep. Dana Rohrabacher (R-CA) told the panel, "we can do more than just sanctions," meaning advocating covert support for Iranian opposition forces "so that they will have the material well-being...to take on that government themselves." From there, Rep. John Boozman (R-AR) proceeded to argue that he will support Israeli bombing of Iran, while Orde Kittrie proposed that it would be better for the United States to carry out any military action because "we have the right capacity."

From imposing "crippling sanctions" to initiating "covert operations," all the way down to military attack by Israel and/or the United States amounts to a familiar scenario that has a very simple and coded antecedent in modern Iranian political culture—the CIA-engineered *coup d'état* of 1953, for which President Obama apologized during his speech at Cairo University in June 2009. Contrary to the vision and wisdom of the president, and as evident in this particular congressional hearing, the political machinations of the US congress and the flawed advice offered by this group of panelists amount to a belligerent threat against the regime, with dire consequences for the grassroots movement inside the country.

To avoid that dangerous route, we need to make a distinction between the nuclear ambitions of the Islamic Republic and the growing civil rights movement in Iran. So far as the nuclear issue is concerned, the only viable and legitimate way to make sure the Islamic Republic does not develop a nuclear weapons program remains a multilateral approach through the International Atomic Energy Agency (IAEA) and geared toward a regional disarmament. This approach must begin by fully recognizing the fact that pursuing a peaceful nuclear program is widely supported by the Iranian people—even by those who regard the election as invalid. Any unilateral approach by the United States that categorically disregards this fact and overlooks the crucial question of regional nuclear disarmament is frightfully reminiscent of the lead-up to the Iraq War and is bound to fail.

So far as the emerging civil rights movement is concerned, there is absolutely not a shred of evidence that any major or even minor opposition leader—from Mousavi to Karroubi to Khatami or any of their related political organs or legitimate representatives—has ever uttered a word that could possibly be interpreted as calling for or endorsing any sort of economic sanction against Iran, let alone "crippling sanction."

As in the Iraqi case, imposition of economic sanctions on Iran will have catastrophic humanitarian consequences, while at the same time it will even more enrich and empower such critical components of the security and military apparatus as the *Pasdaran* and the *Basij*, the combination of which in fact works like a massive corporate conglomerate and has a major control over the export–import components of both the official and the unofficial economy. It will also give them a welcome opportunity to accuse the opposition of cooperation with "the Enemy" and initiate even a harsher crackdown of the opposition, and perhaps even move toward a full-fledged military coup. This is the effective consequence of the congressional hearing, what ever its objective might be in misplacing a trust on a panel of mis-informants. The fact of the matter is that the nascent civil rights movement in Iran, which can always use the moral support of ordinary Americans, is an amorphous uprising still very much in its earliest, formative, stages. No one, particularly a panel that has a very thin and dubious claim on scholarship on Iran, can speak for it in any certain terms—especially in its having asked for imposing economic sanctions on Iranians.

Of one thing though we must all be sure and wary: having scarce come out of the Iraqi quagmire, we need to be exceedingly cautious of the Iranian variations on Ahmed Chalabi, the native informant Iraqi who goaded the American press and the US officials into believing that Iraq had acquired weapons of mass destruction and had links to al-Qaeda, and that the Iraqis would welcome the American army as liberators. He was catastrophically misinformed, when he was not plainly lying.

Not Millions, Just a Quote from MLK Will Do[5]

On a number of occasions and in perfectly pitched and calibrated statements, President Obama has expressed his unequivocal support for the nascent civil rights movement in Iran without appearing to interfere in Iranian domestic affairs. This has been particularly admirable given the pressure that is coming his way from the US congress that up until the night before the Iranian presidential election was discussing even more severe economic sanctions on Iran, which would have hurt precisely the young men and women they now seem too eager to support!

President Obama can help this budding seed of hope for civil liberties even more emphatically by altogether cutting the allocated budget "to promote democracy in Iran," evidently channeled through the United States Agency for International Development (USAID). Ken Dilanian of *USA Today* reports, "the Obama administration is moving forward with plans to fund groups that support Iranian dissidents ("U.S. grants end support to Iran's dissidents," *USA Today*, June 26–28, 2009). This financial aid is not only a waste of taxpayers money, under these severe economic circumstances but is in fact the surest way to kill that inborn and grassroots movement, for it will be mostly abused by expatriate and entirely discredited opposition groups, ranging from the monarchist supporters of Reza Pahlavi to the members of the Mojahedin Khalq Organization, and will in turn strengthen the hand of the regime to denounce the Green Movement as funded by Americans. Not a penny to these groups or any other outlet dedicated to promoting "democracy in Iran" from the sunny coasts of California or the green suburbs of Washington DC.

As the whole world is now a witness to it, the commencement of the civil rights movement in Iran is a nonviolent demand to exercise people's constitutional rights to participate in the democratic aspirations of their homeland, turned bloody only by the custodians of an Islamic Republic that seem to be too conscious of their own illegitimacy. This movement has been decades if not centuries in the making—and it needs no American money to sustain itself. The only thing that it needs is the moral voice of the American Civil Rights Movement to come to its aid. Just one quote from MLK (or more accurately from the prominent nineteenth century abolitionist Theodore Parker) about the arc of the moral universe being long, but ultimately bending toward justice, will go a long way in supporting this movement.

If I were the president, I would reallocate that budget and spend it on faculty development and curricular enrichment of inner city public schools, enabling them to develop courses on modern Iranian and Islamic history. I would convene a national convention, over which the First Lady, Michelle Obama can preside the, and in which public high school teachers will be brought together to think through curricular changes that will teach the next generation of Americans more about the world in which they have to live. From the same fund and the same convention I would establish an annual prize for the 100 best essays written by a Junior from a public high school on contemporary Islamic society, a prize that can be applied to college tuition, and I will call it Rosa Parks-Neda Aqa Soltan Prize for Nonviolent Civil Rights Movement.

Not just one but four swords of Damocles are now hanging over the nascent Iranian civil rights movement. One of them, the severe crackdown by the custodians of the Islamic Republic, has already dropped ruthlessly, and Iranians are more than capable of dodging it and continuing with creative ways of civil disobedience and nonviolent strategies of pushing forward from their versions of the Montgomery Bus Boycott of 1955–1956 to their Civil Rights Act of 1968. But the other three swords are held over this movement from outside Iran, in fact from the US government. These are (1) the misappropriation of funds to "promote democracy in Iran" that will in fact abort it; (2) the fear of even more severe economic sanctions that will do nothing to the ruling elite except for exacerbating its belligerence, while hurting the very brave men and women challenging the brutality of their government; and (3) the threat of military strike that, should it materialize, will have this hopeful uprising as its very first target, while creating the condition of an open military coup in Iran, turning it into another Pakistan.

The United States can only lead, if it must, by example, by practicing what it preaches. Our inner schools cannot suffer from unfathomable poverty of educational tools, and monolingual entrapment within a multicultural world, while we allocate massive millions of dollars to useless, ineffective, discredited, "oppositional" forces. Whatever the fate of the Islamic Republic, the noble cause of civil liberties will remain constant in Iran and will emerge as a model for the region. The memories of the valiant fight put up by Neda Aqa Soltan and Rosa Parks, in the pursuit of freedom from repression, should be inspirational for Iranians and Americans to finally come together in the most enduring virtues of their common dreams of basic human decency—and what better president to have a hand in that union than the man who is a beneficiary of the courage and imagination of Rosa Parks and a witness to Neda Aqa Soltan's?

The White Moderates and the Green Movement[6]

I must confess that over the past few years I have been gravely disappointed with the white moderate. I have almost reached the regrettable conclusion that the Negro's great stumbling block in his stride toward freedom is not the White Citizen's Councilor or the Ku Klux Klanner, but the white moderate, who is more devoted to "order" than to justice; who prefers a negative peace which is the absence of tension to a positive peace which is the presence of justice.

Martin Luther King, Jr., "Letter from a Birmingham Jail" (April 16, 1963)

The only reason why the world at large should take the slightest notice what American pundits think of the Green Movement in Iran is that their self-indulgent punditry reveals much about the troubled world in which we all live, and they think they must lead.

One of the most magnificent aspects of the unfolding civil rights movement (code-named Green) in Iran is that it acts as a catalyst to expose the bizarre banality of American foreign policy punditry and its constitutional limitations on how to deal with the rest of the world. Those in the American foreign policy circles that are of the "bomb bomb Iran" persuasion are lost causes and just like the Ku Klux Klan among the white supremacist scarce need any second look. It is the functional equivalents of what in a different but similar context the late MLK Jr. called "the white moderates" that need more urgent attention.

Perhaps the single most important problem with American politics, policy makers, and pundits—Left or Right, Liberal or Conservative, Democrat or Republican—is that they think anything that happens anywhere in the world is about them, or of their business. It is not. The imperial hubris that seems to be definitive to the DNA of this political culture wants either to invade and occupy other people's homeland and tell them what to do, or else disregard people's preoccupation with their own issues and impose—demand and exact—what they call an "engagement" on them, whether they want it or not.

Take the most recent piece of nonsense published on the civil rights movement in Iran by Flint and Hillary Leverett, "Another Iranian Revolution? Not Likely" (*The New York Times* January 5, 2010), which has absolutely nothing to do or seriously to say about the Green Movement and yet everything to reveal about the pathology of American politics as determined in the self-delusional cocoon inside the Beltway.

As early as mid-June 2009, the Leverett were up and about defending the fraudulent election of Ahmadinejad: "Without any evidence," they charged in an article ("Ahmadinejad won. Get over it," *Politico*, June 15, 2009) that "many U.S. politicians and 'Iran experts' have dismissed Iranian President Mahmoud Ahmadinejad's reelection Friday, with 62.6 percent of the vote, as fraud." That millions of Iranians had also poured into their streets and put their lives on the line with the same charge did not seem to bother the Leveretts. Among those "experts," who had corroborated these charges and supported those demonstrators, and which the Leveretts put into quotation marks by way of denigrating and dismissing them were the leading Iranian scholars in and out of their homeland and the Leveretts will have to come back a few other lifetimes to come anywhere near their competence and knowledge of their homeland.

The Leveretts made a legitimately positive and good name for themselves during the Dark Ages of Bushism by standing up to neoconservative plots to impose more "crippling sanctions" on Iran as a prelude to a military strike. Those of us who recall the nightmare of those years remember the Everetts with an abiding affection and admiration. But this time around, by categorically and condescendingly dismissing a massive civil rights movement altogether, they are falling off the roof from the other side of Bushism—and in doing so they reveal something deeply troubling in American political punditry. It is very disheartening to discredit a courageous couple who in dire circumstances were voices of reason and sanity, and yet they have now fallen victims to their own inability to think outside the proverbial Washington box and ventured into territories dangerously unfamiliar to them.

In addition to a condescending tone, in which the Leveretts speak freely when talking about a groundbreaking civil rights movement about whose origin and disposition they are categorically ignorant, the chief characteristic of their take is that they keep fabricating nonexistent targets and then keep shooting them down. The result: Everything they say has everything to do with the besieged and bunkered mentality inside the Beltway and absolutely nothing to do with the Green Movement.

Chief example: "The Islamic Republic of Iran," they believe, "is not about to implode. Nevertheless, the misguided idea that it may do so is becoming enshrined as conventional wisdom in Washington."

Whoever said it was? No scholar or otherwise serious and informed observer of Iran writing in Persian or any other language and still in her or his right mind can predict or has predicted whether the Islamic Republic will or will not fall, and even if it did, one way or another, it will have nothing to do with what "the conventional wisdom in

Washington" (what ever that oxymoronic phrase may mean) opts to enshrine or not to enshrine. If there are folks inside the Beltway who think that the Islamic Republic will fall any day now, Abbas Milani will become the American ambassador to Iran, or the Iranian ambassador to the United States, depending on the season of his migrations to the Left or Right, and *Lolita* will soon become the required reading in Iranian high schools, This is their problem, and yet another sign of their dangerously delusional politics. That hallucination has nothing to do with the Green Movement, and thus the Leveretts need not have sought (in vain) to discredit a monumental social uprising of whose origin and destination they are entirely innocent.

These Washingtonians live in a world of their own, with little-to-no connection to reality. A massive civil rights movement has commenced in a rich and diversified political culture, and it embraces a wide range of positions and possibilities, of which people trapped inside the Beltway (physically or mentally) have no blasted clue, and thus what American pundits, of one persuasion or another, make of it is entirely irrelevant to its course or consequences. This is a civil rights movement some 200 years in the making, whose very political alphabet is Greek to these folks, and whose course and contour will be determined inside Iran and by Iranians, and not in the halls of power in the United States by American politicians, their pundits, and their contingent of native informers.

No Iranian could care less what people in halls of power in the United States think of their uprising, unless and until they start harming and throwing monkey wrenches at it. There are two sorts of monkey wrenches that they can throw at the Green Movement: (1) economic sanctions, covert operations, and military strike, advocated by one kind of imperial hubris in the United States (aided and abetted by the hunchback Ephialtes of this warlike Empire Abbas Milani), or else (2) engaging with the illegitimate and fraudulent government of Mahmoud Ahmadinejad, as the Leveretts enthusiastically advocate. These are both interferences in the domestic affairs of Iran, of a sovereign nation-state, on the scale and model of the CIA-engineered coup of 1953. Mr. and Mrs. Leveretts ought to know they will be remembered in Iranian history as the twenty-first century versions of Kermit Roosevelt if they persist, as they have since the commencement of the Green Movement in June of last year, in actively siding with what in Iran is called "the coup government of Ahmadinejad."

143

The supreme irony of the Leveretts' position is that while the ghastly propaganda machinery of the Islamic Republic accuses anyone who dares to utter a word against their criminal atrocities to be "an agent of CIA," and here is an (ex-) CIA agent acting as the greatest proponent of their theocratic terrorism.

The Leveretts' concern is with President Obama to hurry up and "engage" with Ahmadinejad before it is too late: "For President Obama, this misconception provides a bit of cover; it helps obscure his failure to follow up on his campaign promises about engaging Iran with any serious, strategically grounded proposals." This concern, to be sure, stems from a legitimate and perhaps even urgent fear that the neocon chicanery of WINEP and Co. that continues to put pressure on Obama administration to pursue a more belligerent path with the Islamic Republic may indeed succeed in doing so, and the Leveretts are particular to preempt that and push the president in the opposite direction and get him involved in diplomacy with Ahmadinejad's administration. That perfectly legitimate and even laudable and noble concern, however, soon degenerates into an arrogant and ignorant dismissal of an entire civil rights movement as something ephemeral and even nonexistent.

The best thing that President Obama has done so far is in fact not to engage with the fraudulent and criminal government of Ahmadinejad, listening carefully to masses of millions of Iranians chanting "Obama, Obama, You are either with them or with us!" And "them" is the brutal theocracy whose security apparatus kidnaps, tortures, rapes, and murders its own citizens, when it is not busy putting their political and intellectual leaders on show trials in Kangaroo courts—facts evidently entirely inconsequential to the Leveretts' *Realpolitik* and yet facts not manufactured by the useless and discredited expatriate opposition groups like the Pahlavi monarchists or the Mojahedin, but facts according to Mehdi Karroubi, Mir-Hossein Mousavi, and Mohammad Khatami, men who have been at the heart of the Islamic Revolution, leading it for the last 30 years, and still deeply committed to the Islamic Republic; and also facts that are admitted by both Mahmoud Ahmadinejad (who in his deranged mind attributes them to "plots by foreigners") and Ali Khamenei (who thinks them less important than his throne).

It would be utterly catastrophic (both for Iranians and for the long term US–Iran relations) if president Obama were to listen to and do as the Leveretts tell him to do—disregard the collective will of a nation demanding and exacting their civil liberties, and engage with a government that sends its security forces to club its own citizens to death, run them over by armored trucks, shoot at them from rooftops, throw them down from bridges, or else point blank and cold-bloodedly murder them. The Leveretts seem to be perfectly cool with this. Standard operation for Third World countries, perhaps they think—well not so by millions of Iranians, if you do not mind.

If President Obama were to ignore the will of millions of Iranians who have over the last 7 months (and not just on the day of Ashura) been pouring into their streets in their millions and screaming *Allahu Akbar* from their rooftops, he will have committed a folly worse than the CIA-sponsored coup of 1953, in which the Leveretts' predecessors prevented the possibility of a democratic Iran more than half a century earlier.

If the Leveretts are opposed to their government's invading other countries and maiming and murdering their people, which is a perfectly noble position to have, they should just do that without interfering in the internal affairs of a sovereign nation that has taken to task the flagrant usurpation of their democratic rights. What the Leveretts are doing is no different from the Neocons, who wish to impose sanction, engage in covert operations, and even launch a military strike against Iran; whereas the Good Samaritan couple wants to impose "engagement" via a total disregard for the manifest will of a people.

The entire argument of the Leveretts dwells on a silly number game they like to play like belligerent teenagers comparing the size of their vanities, all set in a prep school adolescent debating club mentality, questioning the numbers of antigovernment and pro-government rallies. Comparing and contrasting the two massive demonstrations in the holy months of Muharram, one against the government and the other orchestrated by it, the Leveretts sound entirely identical with the propaganda machinery of the Islamic Republic that dismisses one as insignificant and peripheral and celebrates the other as "possibly the largest crowd in the streets of Tehran since Ayatollah Ruhollah Khomeini's funeral in 1989."

In this bogus assessment the Leveretts first and foremost ignore the fact that in one of these two demonstrations people were beaten up, shot at, run over by security officers' armored trucks, or else arrested and taken to the dungeons of the Islamic Republic to be tortured, raped, and murdered (again, according to the past and present officials of the Islamic Republic itself, and for which a former public prosecutor, the notorious Said Mortazavi, is now officially charged and indicted); while in the other they are provided with complementary food and beverages, paraded on national television, and given the day off from work and school.

This is not to suggest that all who went to the staged rally did so just because their livelihood and monthly paychecks were at stake, for their religious sensibilities were equally manipulated in a sinister and abusive game by a vicious and scheming regime. But this entire number game is a silly and useless diversion, and of interest only to discredited expatriate oppositional groups or else to the propaganda machinery of the Islamic Republic, which the Leveretts now echo. Neither all those who participated in the Ashura demonstrations wish to topple the Islamic Republic nor are all those who were manipulated to join the counter demonstrations are supporters of Ahmadinejad. This entire fixation with numbers is played on the false field of a supposition that this is a revolution in the making, or the Islamic Republic is about to fall, whereas for the last 7 months anyone who knows anything about Iran (and none of them seems to be in the vicinity of Washington DC) has insisted that this is NOT a revolution, but (as I have said since day one) a civil rights movement and a marathon (though a wrong metaphor for Iran) rather than a 100 m sprint. It is the self-conscious custodians of the Islamic Republic, always overtly aware of their illegitimacy, that after every major or minor national election blasts its loudspeakers with assurances that people have actually voted and lo and behold how legitimate they are.

Another equally useless game and diversionary goose chase that the Leveretts play, a game that shows they are completely out of their elements when it comes to understanding this movement (or at least they should hire a better native informer), is when they start talking about the seventh day memorial of one death or another. People, please just have some decency and stop making pseudo orientalist fools of yourselves! There is more than one way to skin a cat.

What happened in the seventh day commemoration of Grand Ayatollah Montazeri's death on December 27, 2009, which coincided with the Ashura on 10th of the holy month of Muharram 1431 in the Islamic calendar, is integral to a succession of mass rallies that began on June 12 and has taken any occasion—from Jerusalem Day (September 18), to the anniversary of the American Hostage Crisis (November 4), to Student Day (December 7), the funeral of Grand Ayatollah Montazeri

(December 21), and to Ashura (December 27)—to pour into streets, demand and exact their rightful public space, and show their discontent with this brutal banality that has suffocated and abused them for more than three decades. Come next anniversary of the Islamic Revolution in February, or the next *Chahar Shanbeh Suri*, *Noruz*, or *Sizdah Bedar* (ask your native informer what these are) in March, people will do exactly the same. And these are not the only ways to show civil disobedience—in the making of a civil rights movement, *not* a revolution. The Islamic Republic may or may not last, under pressure from its own internal contradictions that it may or may not be able to rectify. But that possibility, or even eventuality, is entirely irrelevant to the civil liberties that this movement is demanding and will exact from this or any other regime. To understand that last sentence, you ought to get out of Washington DC and brush up with a couple of courses on modern Iranian history in a half-decent college.

The Leveretts are led to believe that their trump cards are three earth-shattering questions they need answered by those who believe something extraordinary is happening in Iran. Let us bracket for the moment the fact that judging by this piece of writing these folks are simply not qualified to ask the right and intelligent questions about this movement and humor them. "Those who talk so confidently about an 'opposition' in Iran as the vanguard for a new revolution," they say, putting the word "opposition" in quotation mark by way of belittling, ridiculing, and dismissing it, "should be made to answer three tough questions: First, what does this opposition want? Second, who leads it? Third, through what process will this opposition displace the government in Tehran?"

Well, for one thing, they should really shop around for a better native informer (or simply swap him or her for a Google translator) for the one who has told them that Mir-Hossein Mousavi had criticized radical acts during the Ashura should have also told them that the whole world and their extraterrestrial counterparts know by now that the triumvirate of Mousavi, Karroubi, and Khatami collectively constitute the core of what literate observers have called, in Persian of course, *rahbari-ye ghaltan*, a "rotating leadership."

This is Green Movement leadership question 101. Now at a slightly more advanced level outside the Beltway IQ level, the nature of "leadership" in this movement is not, as the Leveretts assume, on the revolutionary model of Khomeini in 1979, for that would be the scenario of a revolutionary leadership, and not the leadership of the sustained

147

course of a civil rights movement, the way that from Homer Plessy to Medgar Evers to Rosa Parks to MLK Jr. to Malcolm X were the leaders of the Civil Rights movement in the United States. But the trouble with these "white moderates," as MLK Jr. would call them, is that they cannot think of a country like Iran having a civil rights movement, for perhaps they have never come to terms with the one in their own country, and thus in their estimation oriental folks are only capable of either a revolution or a military coup—that is all the colored folks are capable of doing. If they were to drop their condescending orientalist guards and look and learn carefully, the good Leveretts would see that this movement has plenty of leaders, not all of them men, not all of them "religious intellectuals," as they call themselves. But that would be too advanced a seminar if the Leveretts' essay were to be taken as the measure of intelligence in what "Washingtonians" know about this movement.

As for what the movement wants, again any native informer with a slight command over Persian should have told the Leveretts that in the selfsame statement Mousavi has specified five very clear objectives, which objectives were subsequently extended into ten even more specific items—ranging from the resignation of Ahmadinejad to freeing all political prisoners and unconditional freedom of the press—by five leading "religious intellectuals" in a historic document that every Iranian and their cousins around the globe are now discussing, but it has evidently been kept hidden from the Leveretts.

As to the third question of how this is to happen, again Mohsen Kadivar, a leading clerical opponent of the Islamic Republic who despite his young age is in fact superior in his juridical rank and learning to the "leader" of the Islamic Republic, has just told *Le Monde* very specifically, in three itemized moves, how they are going to achieve their ends. In this interview, Kadivar recommends a referendum with three options: (1) an Islamic Republic without *Velayat Faqih*, a Republic minus the adjective Islamic, or else the Islamic Republic with *Velayat Faqih*. As in any other civil rights movement, Kadivar of course does not speak for the whole movement. But in terms of the kinds of objectives that are now on the table, his language is certainly in the main ballpark.

But the ultimate problem with the three wrong questions the Leveretts ask is that they, and their adversaries in Washington DC, not the Green Movement itself, are debating whether this is a revolution or not. That is their problem, which they are fighting on the back of someone else's civil rights movement.

The problem with American pundits, as they are called, is that their warmongers impose wars and their liberals wish to demand and exact "engagements"—but both irrespective of the fact that sovereign nations should neither be invaded by imperial armies nor be interrupted with "engagement" when they are busy attending to some housecleaning of their own. It is as simple as inviting yourself to someone's house, when they are in the middle of a family feud. It is simply rude.

Based on this prototypical example, the American intelligence community could use a bit of theorizing, returning the anthropological gaze "the West" has always cast around the world. There is a reason that a gargantuan security and intelligence apparatus, magnified by billions of more dollars after 9/11, is still so incompetent, as just angrily admitted by President Obama, that it could not even prevent a deranged mind like Umar Farouk Abdulmutallab boarding a plane headed to the United States, when the man's own father had approached the US and Nigerian authorities telling them that his son was about to commit a terrorist act. The problem with the Leveretts' shortsighted tunnel vision is thus not exclusive to them; it is endemic to the American intelligence community and political punditry. Their failure in understanding the civil rights movement in Iran is ultimately predicated on the fact that at its best their thinking is merely mechanical (not organic), systematically synchronic (and never simultaneously diachronic). Instead of seeing things in organically diachronic long terms, they are all afflicted with seeing things in mechanically synchronic short term.

Consider, for example, the Leveretts' most obvious blind spot. They are very particular to inform people that there is no popular revolution in the offing that may topple the Islamic Republic—and yet fail to notice that the Islamic Republic is in fact far more in danger of a naked military coup by the Revolutionary Guards, following what millions of Iranians (including the very founders of the Islamic Republic) believe to have been an electoral coup. What about that possibility? Should the Obama administration also deal with a military junta (as it does in Pakistan), while a massive civil rights moment is unfolding. None of these realities and even worse possibilities, not even the criminal obscenity of rape, torture, and murder, seem to bother the Leveretts. Very bizarre—how is this *Realpolitik* different from becoming a mouthpiece for a fanatical theocratic absolutism? Is that because Iranians are thought not to deserve or not to know any better? Are the Leveretts ready to face the charge of white supremacist racism—that a fanatical absolutism is *"Bon pour L'Orient,"* as the old Belgian colonial catechism used to put it?

What is happening in Iran *is* a "revolution," though in a sense not entirely conceivable in the captured imagination either of the medieval theocracy that is ruling Iran or by the even more archaic Cold War mentality of the Leveretts (judged by their reference to Nixon and China as a model for Obama and Iran). For what is happening in Iran is a revolution not in a mundane politics of despair but a revolution in *form*, in *language*, in *style*, in *decorum*, in *demeanor*, and in visual and performative *sublimity*. This is a movement that began with song and dance, with poetry and drama, with color and choreography, with joy, laughter, and hope, with an open-ended hermeneutics of what is possible beyond the written text, or the spoken word, or the mandated morality, or the legislated signs—no matter which candidate people preferred and voted for. This civil rights movement will change the very alphabet of the region, from form to content, from rhetoric to logic, from Iran to the rest of the region, across the Arab and Muslim world, and then beyond. Student activists from Ohio to Beijing are learning from their Iranian counterparts. In inner city schools around New York there is a new idiom, "going Iranian," meaning not remaining passive in the face of nonsense? None of these still matters for policymakers and pundits to measure in any "University of Maryland Survey." But put your ears to the ground and you will hear it grumble. This movement is iconoclastic, puts veils on men's head, places women in the front row of rallies, showers cool water and love over the security forces that come to beat up their own brothers and sisters.

But all of that is beyond the bunkered banality that passes for punditry in the United States. To speak in the language interior to the Beltway, there is not an iota of difference between Bush's waging war on Afghanistan and Iraq and the Leveretts' recommendation of an imperial decree for "engagement" with the Islamic Republic, no matter what diabolic regime flaunts a claim on that dubious epithet. But the good news is that Iranians could not care less either about the hawks or the doves mixing their own metaphors and interfering in other people's business. If the Leveretts want to fight against their country's immoral, illegal, and fattening warmongering around the world, they have their work cut out for them inside their own country. They have no business imposing their imperial prescription on a people busy doing some housecleaning of their own. Whether this Green Movement attains its objective a year form now or 10 years from now, whether the Islamic Republic will accommodate those civil liberties and survive or fails to do so and joins other political dinosaur museums is none of Leveretts' business, or the American government's for that matter. A people, once again, have risen to demand and exact their civil liberties. So please, if you do not mind, just step aside.

Notes

1. An earlier version of this essay appeared on CNN.com (November 4, 2009).
2. An earlier version of this essay appeared on CNN.com (October 1, 2009).
3. An earlier version of this essay was published as "A Tale of Two Cities" in *al-Ahram* (August 20, 2009).
4. An earlier version of this essay appeared as "Huge risks in Iran sanctions" in CNN.com (August 5, 2009).
5. An earlier version of this essay was published as "U.S. dollars could kill Iran's protest movement" in CNN.com (June 30, 2009).
6. An earlier version of this essay was published as "White moderates and greens" in *al-Ahram Weekly* (January 21–27, 2010).

7

The Green Movement, the Palestinian Cause, and Racism

The Arab Roaming in the Streets of Tehran[1]

In Memoriam
Ardeshir Mohassess (1938–2008)
Cartoonist:
Historian of our fears and frivolities

It was late at night, and quite tired after a long day I was hanging out with a number of Palestinian filmmaker friends in front of Khalil Sakkakini Cultural Center in Ramallah. It was late in February 2004. I was waiting for Annemarie Jacir to finish her chores introducing the films we were screening that night and to come down so we could go for a late night dinner with our friends from Yabous Productions, an East Jerusalem-based Palestinian art organization that was hosting us.

Annemarie and I were in Ramallah for the Palestinian wing of the film festival, "Dreams of a Nation," we had earlier organized in New York in January 2003. In Palestine, we were screening films in Jerusalem, Ramallah, Bethlehem, Nazareth, Nablus, and Gaza City. We were elated. The weather was cool, the air crisp, and the breeze across the West Bank quite pleasant. It reminded me of the summer nights of Ahvaz, though this was still in February in Palestine. Israeli military jeeps were patrolling the Sakkakini Foundation neighborhood in an inconspicuous way. The soldiers looked like GI Joe figurines—their quiet plasticity visibly robotic. The jeeps cruised quietly around us like they were driving themselves, or else guided by some sort of remote control, a playful child maneuvering them from behind an olive tree nearby for our amusement. A powerful floodlight was lighting the terrace in front of the Sakkakini Foundation. We were all quietly happy.

153

"You are Iranian, right," the young Palestinian filmmaker standing next to me asked, Raed was his name, a soft smile looked like having been carved at birth on his youthful face. Yes, I said, I am. "What are you doing here," he wondered, with a certain metaphysical tone in his voice, as in, of all places, what are you doing in this particular place. He was not expecting any answer, as if knowing what the answer was, but airing it gave him a certain playful satisfaction. A refreshing and cool breeze was in the air. I felt pleasantly chilled, happy, giddy even. There was a pleasing wonder in Raed's voice, punctuated by a knowing smile. Nothing, I said, answering his metaphysics with the only negative dialectic I know.

People were walking out of the small theater inside Sakkakini Foundation. The films we were showing—I think, they were a couple of Elia Suleiman's shots—were just finished. "You have come all the way here," Raed continued with his merriment at the heel of my disarming casuistry, "to show us films?" He was a master of emotive dissonance. His face betrayed his frivolity. When I said yes because you have not seen these films, he just widened his face with a bigger, warmer, more reassuring smile. I thought I had been an object of curiosity for him; he acted as if he was directing me in a Fellini film—tongue in cheek—despite myself.

Annemarie came down and was busy chatting with some of the people in the audience. I saw Adania Shibli behind her—a young Palestinian poet I had come to know and admire during that trip. Behind Adania Shibli was Miguel Littin, the Chilean–Palestinian filmmaker who had come all the way from Santiago to be with us during the festival. "Here," Raed turned to me as he reached deep inside the front pocket of his jeans and pulled out his keychain. He carefully took his keys out of the ring and handed me the keychain, from which was hanging a small statuette. "Here is your Oscar!"

Keys are very powerful objects for Palestinians. They symbolize and represent their lost, confiscated, stolen, and occupied homes. What was holding Raed's keys together was no less powerful a symbol.

I took the keychain and looked at the small statuette. Initially I could not tell what it was. It took me a few seconds to figure out it was Hanzala. "Do you know who he is," Raed wondered, having just handed me my Oscar. Yes I do, I said. Thanks. "He is a witness," he said, "just like you!"

Not many non-Palestinians know who Hanzala is. Hanzala is the legendary creation of Naji Salim al-Ali (1938–1987), a Palestinian cartoonist, known, loved, and celebrated for a sustained body of works that has survived him with astounding power and tenacity. Estimates are that he drew nearly 50,000 cartoons, in which he documented various phases of the Palestinian national liberation struggle. He was as much, if not more, critical of spineless Arab leaders as he was of Israeli occupation of his homeland. Born in Palestine, raised in Ain Al-Helwa refugee Camp in Southern Lebanon, he eventually emerged as the visual conscience of his people. Before he was assassinated on July 22, 1987 and died a few weeks later in London, Naji al-Ali had immortalized the figure of Hanzala: solitary, serious, single-mindedly determined to be a witness to his people's history.

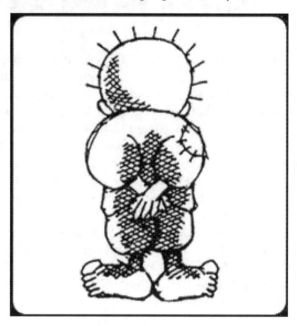

Hanzala is by far the most famous persona in Palestinian visual and emotive vocabulary—a curious and persistent figurine who stands witness to the suffering and struggles of his people. He is, above all, a witness, an eyewitness, to be exact, a muse of conscience, commanding us to act, with his back turned to us, as if he is leading us forward, toward the scene, where history is happening. He just stands there, with his back toward us, the spectators, and facing the scene of the crime, or the struggle, or the atrocity, or the defiance. His back facing us is also accusatory—what are you doing, just standing there watching; it is as if he is saying—what is there to watch? Why do not you join us in, come in, into the picture, into history, where the action is, the injustice, the struggle, where we, where he, where what he witnesses, needs your help, at least your testimony. Hanzala is testimonial.

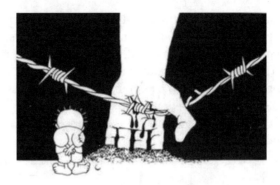

Disregarding us, Hanzala is watching. Nothing escapes his attention. We do not see his face or his eyes, because his face is turned away from us and toward the scene of the crime, and his eyes are fixated on what he is watching, what needs watching, what the criminals do not want anyone to see. The Palestinian history of invisibility, of denial, is at the heart of Hanzala's visual fixation. But even beyond Palestine, Hanzala is the moral mind's eyes watching that which is made invisible. Our eyes wide shut, his are wide open—and yet, and there is the rub, we cannot see his eyes, for he is in our eyes, he is our eyes, mediated through the distanced space that holds us back from where he stands, right in front of the event, where history is happening. Single-handedly, Hanzala sees our hesitant bets and raises it by his courage.

Hanzala does not just watch and bear testimony. He also acts. He picks up a pen and draws, and a stone and throws. He lights a candle. He defies submission. Hanzala persists. He never gives up.

Hanzala has survived the death of his creator Naji al-Ali and continues to lead a thriving, engaged, and committed life where he is most needed—not just in Palestine, anywhere else where he is needed. I have an "anti-globalization" T-shirt someone once gave me, with a picture of Hanzala! When during the summer of 2004, I was traveling through the Palestinian refugee camps in Lebanon, I saw the power of the living memory of Naji al-Ali, in the figure of his Hanzala adorning the walls and banners of Palestinians in their direst moments and most defiant aspirations. Walking through these camps, you will see many replicas of Hanzala informing, assuring, warning, admonishing, leading on, or encouraging the residents to do one thing or another. He grew up in refugee camps. He knows them inside out, and deeply cares for their inhabitants. I remember once in Badawi Refugee Camp up in northern Lebanon near Tripoli, we screened Rashid Mashharawi's "A Ticket to Jerusalem" (2002) on the rooftop of The United Nations Relief and Work Agency (UNERWA) building and onto a wall upon which stood Hanzala, his back turned to us as he was writing on the white wall, *al-Qods Lana/Jerusalem is ours*. On another occasion in Shatila Refugee Camp in Beirut I had seen Hanzala putting his signature under a statement over a pile of garbage that had not been collected yet: *Hafezu ala Nezafat al-Mokhayyim* or *Look after the Sanitation of the Camp*.

Born in Palestine, raised in a refugee camp in Lebanon, Naji al-Ali and Hanzala, the creator and the character traveled deep and wide into the world and made of *Intifada*, of uprising against tyranny, a transnational metaphor. Hanzala is and remains Palestinian, but he is also metamorphosed into a global metaphor, a visual trope, a witness everywhere, just like John Steinbeck's Tom Joad: "Whenever they's a fight so hungry people can eat, I'll be there. Whenever they's a cop beatin' up a guy, I'll be there ... I'll be in the way guys yell when they're mad an'-I'll be in the way kids laugh when they're hungry" That visual universality remains rooted in the Palestinian predicament and defiant spirit, but then it goes global in its powerful implications.

A racist rumor is now roaming through the streets of Tehran (exacerbated by even more racist instigations by monarchists from abroad)—that among the security forces beating up on the demonstrators are people who do not speak Persian, that they speak Arabic, that they are dark skinned and thus not Iranian—from Lebanon, Palestine, or Iraq. The whitewashed imagination of those who make up these stories has habitually dismissed Iranians from the southern climes of their homeland as "Arabs," as if being Arab was a misdemeanor. This fictive foreigners beating up and killing Iranians used to be Afghan when millions of Afghan refugees fled their homeland and sought refuge in Iran in the 1980s; and have now become Arabs. The same racist imagination in and out of Iran now seeks to fish in this muddy water. They have no clue that the only Arab I know for a fact is now roaming the streets of Iran is Hanzala, watching over his Iranian brothers and sisters, a witness to their courage and imagination—blessing their *Intifada*, teaching them a trick or two. Once in a Palestinian refugee camp I met an Iranian warrior, fighting for Palestinians. His *nom de guerre* was Abu Said, for he had named himself after our martyred poet Said Soltanpour (1940–1981). He spoke his Arabic with an enduring Persian accent, and his Persian with Arabic intonations. So does Hanzala, if he were to speak. But he only watches, witnesses, and keeps a record. He holds the key to my home too—a colored southern boy, a born-and-bred Iranian, an honorary Arab, and a Palestinian at heart.

Beyond borders and across linguistic divides, Hanzala lives, breathes, thrives, warns, watches, witnesses, and keeps a record, for the whole world to see. He is everywhere: From the forgotten fury of young and old men and women suffering the indignity of exile in Palestinian refugee camps in Lebanon, to the bruised bodies of defenseless mothers and children in Gaza, to the wounded soul of widows and orphans in Iraq, to the broken bones of humanity in Afghanistan, and then down to the murdered youth and the beaten and broken bodies of young and beautiful protestors in the streets of Iran, assuring them all that he is watching, witnessing, keeping a record, his accusatory back turned to our shame, writing on the walls of Tehran "*Thawra hatta al-Nasr/Qiyam ta Piruzi/Uprising until Victory!*"

Note

1. An earlier version of this essay was published in *Tehran Bureau* (July 7, 2009).

8

Islamic Republic
Tactics in
Staging Legitimacy

Staging a Spontaneous Rally[1]

On December 30, 2009, the Ahmadinejad government staged a massive pro-government demonstration in major Iranian cities. His extensive propaganda machinery, abusing the financial resources that belong to Iranian people, called the spectacle a "spontaneous" show of support for the legitimacy of the Islamic Republic, which word, almost instantly in the cyberspace, gave rise to a concocted Persian neologism: "spontaneous-ed" (*khod-jushandeh*).

People around the globe who saw this carnival might, on the surface, be led to believe that Ahmadinejad's government, and by extension the Islamic Republic that he now represents, is in fact widely popular, and that the Green Movement represents a small minority of Iranian, or that at the very least Iranian society is deeply divided. It is not—and it is imperative to understand why.

Soon after the Islamic Revolution of 1977–1979, some 30 years ago, my colleague Peter Chelkowski and I began collecting an extensive archive of visual material—ranging from posters and murals to elementary school textbooks and even chewing gum wraps—that were effectively used to color and characterize a multifaceted cosmopolitan revolution exclusively "Islamic." It took us more than a decade to collect our archive and publish our "Staging a Revolution: The Art of Persuasion in the Islamic Republic," in which we demonstrated how the custodians of the Islamic Republic went into excruciating detail making sure not a single person waking up in the morning was not exposed to a bombardment of visual propaganda before s/he goes back to bed.

That book is now out of print and something of a collectors' item for the non-Islamist (nationalist and socialist). Visual material we had used to show the alternative visual registers of the uprising were later systematically destroyed, and an excessively Islamist memory was manufactured for the revolution. Be that as it may, we have, at least for the scholarly community, if not for the public at large, massively documented the varied forms in which this particular regime is capable of manufacturing the illusion of popularity for itself.

What the custodians of the Islamic Republic did on Wednesday 30 December 2009 was nothing new, a wrinkled up page from an old and banal book that has after 30 years of abuse lost all effectiveness and use. The formula is very simple and has always been the surest sign of the insecurity of the regime and its overtly conscious awareness that it lacks legitimacy. Public schools and governmental ministries were all told that they have the day off and that buses were available to take them to the location of the rally—food and drink freely provided. Nongovernmental agencies and private companies were told that they would lose lucrative governmental contracts, if they did not dispatch their employees to the rallies. The exams scheduled for Thursday were even canceled so that students will not have any homework or assignment worries as they chanted "death to Mousavi." Religious seminaries from around the country were also mobilized. The squares were carefully selected and the location of the cameras for national television judiciously selected to magnify the size of the crowd. Some very crude modes of editing the films would intercut the direction of the crowd moving into and out of the squares, as if they were part of the same mass of "millions" matching. Dramatic music and pompous newscasters were in charge of manufacturing a phenomenally spontaneous event. Given the extraordinary clumsiness of the event, one can only think that there are green sympathizers at national television, making sure people understand that this is all bogus.

My generation of Iranians remember only too well how in the late 1950s, early 1960s, as school children we were told to report to school at the crack of dawn when His Imperial Majesty, the late Shah of Iran came to Ahvaz and we were bussed to the airport to wave our little flags for him and cheer to show how happy we were to welcome him to our city. In less than two decades, those very young and impressionable kids were out in the streets shouting "Death to the Shah!"

The difference between now and then, or even between now and when the Islamic Revolution was engineered is the miracle of the internet. Within minutes after national television staged its ludicrous show, the internet was flooded with contrary arguments: the difference between people's rallies and the government's rallies. In one, the police beats you up, shoots at you, and throws tear gas at you; in the other they provide you with bus, food and drink, and redirect the traffic for you; in one people are killed, and in the other people pretend they are ready to die; in one the reporters go to jail if they cover it; in the other they get promotions and bonus; in one millions are numbered thousands; in the other thousands millions.

None of these is to suggest that Ahmadinejad and his clerical godfathers have no popular support. They do. People's livelihood and monthly paycheck depends on taking part in such carnivals of insecurity and banality. And the louder these rallies scream, the better the world knows how totally aware of their illegitimacy they are.

Note

1.   An earlier version of this essay was published as "Iran's pro-government rallies fool nobody" in CNN.com (January 7, 2010).

Index

Abdulmutallab, Umar Farouk, 149
Abrahamian, Ervand, 105
Abtahi, Ali, 27–28, 81, 84
Abukhalil, As'ad, 99–104
Afary, Janet, 112
Afghanistan
  as a "just war," 120
  recognizing Ahmadinejad
    government, 28
  refugee presence in Iran, 158
  revenge, 91
  Taliban influence, 66, 79, 124
  US presence in, 54, 59, 80, 85–86, 98,
    124, 133, 150
Ahmadinejad, Mahmoud
  artists against, 57
  Berlusconi, Silvio, comparisons to,
    116, 119, 121
  chants and slogans, 33, 35, 123
  charlatanism, 26, 61, 83, 99, 108–109,
    119, 135
  debate with Mousavi, 62
  election results, 23–26, 28, 36, 55,
    59, 81
  Holocaust denial, 38, 108, 114
  hypocrisy, 102
  illegitimacy of government, 35, 41,
    100, 143, 161
  Israel favoring, 34, 63–64
  Katie Couric interview, 125–127
  Leveretts' defense of, 141–144
  Obama and, 40–41, 44, 144
  resignation, calling for, 148
  staged rallies, 25, 28, 33, 37, 146,
    161–163
  subsidies to the poor, 61, 108, 114,
    116
  supporters

Ahmadinejad, Mahmoud (continuded)
  among the poor, 25, 56, 105–106,
    110–111, 116–117
  from the Left, 99, 114
  unemployment, 25, 38, 61,
    106–107, 111
al-Ali, Naji Salim, 154–158
Al Arabiya, 101–102
Aliabadi, Shirin, 49
Alikhani, Qodratollah, 26, 33
Allahu Akbar as slogan, 26–28, 52,
  114–115, 145
al-Qaeda, 124, 138
Amanat, Abbas, 109–110
American Hostage Crisis, 67, 76–77, 79,
  118, 123–125, 146
American Israel Public Affairs
  Committee (AIPAC), 62–64, 99
Amnesty International, 82, 94
Arabi, Sohrab, 87
art, Iranian, 46–49, 65, 102
Ashura demonstrations, 40, 145–147
Assembly of Experts, 61, 76
Azari, Shoja, 45, 48

Baha'is, 94–96
Basiji, 9, 69, 107–108, 138
Bazargan, Mehdi, 76
BBC, 25, 27, 30–32, 34
Behesht-e Zahra cemetery, 90
Beltway opinions, 141–143,
  147–148, 150
Berman, Howard, 128, 136
bin Laden, Osama, 52, 124
Bishara, Azmi, 97, 104–105, 107–108
blogs
  Abtahi as popular subject, 81, 84
  of As'ad AbuKhalil, 102

blogs (*continued*)
  bloggers as inspirers, 104
  execution, bloggers threatened with, 33
  of Fatemeh Shams, 93
  Imam Ali mentions, 91–92
  Iran Democracy Project, interest in, 132
  passage from blogger, 86
  wired to globalized world, 65
Boozman, John, 130–131, 137
Burton, Dan, 130, 137
Bush, George W.
  Christian Empire building, 85
  destruction in Iranian environs, 43, 59, 62, 150
  Islamophobia, 95
  Leveretts in Bush era, 142
  presidency as nightmare, 98
  war on terror, 52, 133–134

Carter, Jimmy, 77
Chalabi, Ahmad, 135, 138
Chelkowski, Peter, 161–162
CIA, 98–103, 106, 132, 144, 149 *See also* coup of 1953 *under* coups
cinema, Iranian, 46, 50, 53, 65, 68, 74
civil disobedience, 25–26, 29, 37, 69, 112, 140, 146–147
civil rights movement. *See also* Green Movement
  art and, 48
  compared to that of the US, 112, 148
  determining fate of Islamic Republic, 88
  domino effect, 44
  goal of, 70
  green as symbolic color, 84, 141
  as ground zero, 39, 43
  Hoover Institution, thwarting, 133
  Leveretts' opinion on, 141–142, 144
  Milani as enemy of, 128, 135
  nonviolent, 65, 70, 84, 86, 123, 139–140
  Obama supporting, 138–139
  resulting from June 2009 elections, 39, 43, 90, 128
  revolution, compared to, 53, 65–66, 146–148, 150
  sanctions, no call for, 137–138
Clawson, Patrick, 130, 136

Clinton administration, 98, 134
CNN, 29, 32, 51, 101, 114
Cohen, Roger, 124–125
colonialism
  28-Mordadism, 74, 77
  absolutism, 150
  AbuKhalil, colonized mindset of, 102
  Ahmadinejad on, 108
  anti-colonial nationalism, 45, 65, 67, 78–79, 90
  colonial conditions of Iran, 68
  colonial intellectuals, 120
  Israeli colonialism, 60, 64, 109, 120
  providing the term "Middle East," 85, 97
The Concept of the Political (Schmitt), 134
constitution
  constitutional assembly, 61, 70, 75–76
  Constitutional Revolution of 1906–1911, 66, 74, 85
  constitutional rights, 96, 100, 103–104, 139
  Mousavi restoring, 88
  religious minorities protection, 95–96
coups
  coup of 1953
    28-Mordadism, 73–77
    fear of repeat, 124–125
    Kermit Roosevelt and, 132, 143
    Obama, apology for, 137
    preventing democracy in Iran, 145
    Stephen Kinzer, account of, 100
    traumatic memories, 40, 65
  electoral, 55, 143, 149
  military, 52–53, 70, 138, 140, 148
  Nojeh coup attempt, 77
  velvet, 128, 131–132, 135
Couric, Katie, 125–127
covert operations, 130–131, 133–137, 143–145

Dabashi, Hamid
  during American Hostage Crisis, 123
  emersion in Iranian arts, 46, 50
  Islamic Liberation Theology: Resisting the Empire, 51
  June 2009 election diary, 23–24, 24–26, 26–32, 32–40

Dabashi, Hamid (*continued*)
  the Left, sharing view of, 98
  Masters and Masterpieces of Iranian Cinema, 46
  partnership with Peter Chelkowski, 161–162
  preference for Mousavi, 29, 119
  preoccupations of, 120
  as Shiite Muslim, 32
  Staging a Revolution, 161–162
  Theology of Discontent, 45–46
Death chants, 123, 125, 162
December 30, 2009 demonstrations, 161–163
democracy
  American promotion irrelevant, 55
  from below, 58
  demanding democratic rights, 56
  democratic aspirations, 24, 92
  as grassroots movement, 59, 63–64, 88, 135
  Israel's claim as sole democracy in region, 54
  June 2009 elections as sign of, 131
  promotion of, 139–140

Ebtehaj, Houshang, 93
Erlich, Reese, 98
espionage, 94, 100, 132
Evin prison, 82, 92, 113, 121
expatriates
  academics, 110
  discredited, 87, 139, 144, 146
  monarchists, 63
  quixotic, 84, 93
  women authors, 59

Facebook, 40, 57, 64, 66–68. *See also* Internet
Fanon, Frantz, 45, 114, 120
Farroukhzad, Forough, 46, 69, 74
fascism, 57, 61, 83, 116, 134
Fayyazi, Bita, 48
Fischer, Michael, 53
Foucault, Michel, 103, 113, 115, 118–120
Freudian analysis, 117–118

Ganji, Akbar, 29, 83
Gaza, 80, 82–83, 86, 98, 108, 153, 158
green color symbolism

green color symbolism (*continued*)
  adopted by Mousavi camp, 28, 52, 58, 65, 67, 114–115
  bandanas/scarves, 36, 45, 53, 66, 69
  multisignatory, 67–68, 70
  showing solidarity with the opposition, 27, 84
Green Movement. *See also* civil rights movement
  accusation of American funding, 139
  American opinions on, 141–143, 149–151
  code name, 66, 141
  expatriate opposition, 94
  leadership, 25–26, 44–45, 78, 84, 147–148
  media sympathizers, 162
  Milani damaging, 135
  nonviolence, 92–93
  not ceasing with end of Islamic Republic, 39
  slogan, 81
  small minority, perceived as, 161
  threats to, 40–41, 80
  voices of, 39, 68
Guardian Council, 28, 33–34, 37, 56, 61

Haaretz, 34, 43, 105
Habermas, Jürgen, 113, 117, 135
Hajjarian, Said, 27–28, 83, 100
Hanzala, 154–158
Hariri, Saad, 54, 109
Hezbollah, 35, 43–44, 54, 76, 79, 109
Hoagland, Eric, 111–112
Hoover Institution, 24, 128, 132–134, 136
Hossein, Saddam, 65, 77, 79, 124
Huntington, Samuel, 51

Imam Ali, 91–92
Imam Hossein, 52
International Atomic Energy Agency (IAEA), 137
Internet. *See also* blogs
  bringing down walls, 51
  connecting youth to global context, 56–57, 65–67
  cyberspace rebellion, 39–40
  December 30, 2009 demonstrations, debate over, 162–163
  Facebook, 40, 57, 64, 66–68

Internet. *See also* blogs (*continued*)
  government shut down, 32
  June 2009 election reactions, 58
  Muslim world watching Iranian use
    of, 64
  threats to users, 33
  Twitter, 33–34, 40, 57, 64, 66–67
  You Tube, 66, 68
Intifada, 63, 79, 104, 157–158
Iran Democracy Project, 24, 132,
  134–136
Iranophobia (Ram), 55
Iran Refined Petroleum Sanctions Act,
  136
Iraq
  8-day war, 77
  Chalabi misinformation, 138
  Iran-Iraq (1980-1988) war, 11, 25,
    38, 62, 67, 79, 124
  sanctions, 134
  US occupation, 54, 59, 80, 85, 115,
    124
*Islamic Liberation Theology: Resisting the
  Empire* (Dabashi), 51
Islamic Republic. *See also* constitution;
  security forces; theocracy; *Velayat-e
  Faqih;* violence
  28-Mordadism, 74–77
  apologists, 129
  crisis mismanagement, 67
  December 30, 2009 demonstrations,
    161–163
  democracy not incompatible with,
    88
  discrimination against minorities,
    94–96
  dismantling, 92
  distorting cosmopolitan culture, 67
  enemies, 68, 131, 133–134, 138
  illegitimacy of
    Ahmadinejad government as
      illegitimate, 35, 41, 100, 143, 161
    crisis of legitimacy, 87, 89–92, 94
    elections not lending legitimacy,
      23, 39, 55, 60, 146
    Green Movement challenging, 38
    insecurity, 107–108, 162
    regional crises, taking advantage
      of, 80
    self-consciousness, 82, 133, 135,
      139, 146, 163

Islamic Republic (*continued*)
  Leveretts' opinion on, 142–144
  military strikes, proposed, 98, 131,
    133–136, 140
  Nazi Germany, compared to, 130,
    137
  nuclear agenda, 40–41, 44, 129–130,
    137
  Pakistan, compared to, 140
  Palestine, expanding presence in, 79
  paranoia of, 133–135
  provincialism, 127
  public opinion against, 126
  self-destructive, 82, 85
  Taliban look-alikes, 91
  totalitarian disposition, 104
  voting on next phase of, 70
  Western conspiracy against, 132
Islamization, 32, 45, 76–78, 89,
  118–119
Islamophobia, 32, 88, 95–96
Israel
  Ahmadinejad candidacy, favoring,
    34, 63–64
  colonialism, 60, 64, 109, 120
  fanatical regimes, 108–109
  Gaza invasion, 80, 108
  Iranian events, exploiting, 99
  Israeli military, 153
  Lebanon invasion, 79–80, 86
  military strikes, threatening, 55, 58,
    70, 98, 130–131, 137
  nuclear concerns, 129, 131
  Palestine, contra, 83, 98
  racism, 54, 59, 109
  Zionists, 58–60, 82–83, 85–86, 91,
    116, 131

Jacir, Annemarie, 153–154
Jala'ipour, Mohammadreza, 93
June 2009 presidential election
  28-Mordadism, 74–75
  civil disobedience, sparking, 25, 37,
    66
  civil rights movement, reaction to,
    39, 43, 90, 128
  coup d'état, 55
  Dabashi diary, 23–24, 24–26, 26–32,
    32–40
  Leveretts' defense of, 141
  losers, 25, 60–63

June 2009 presidential election
(*continued*)
 questioning results, 35, 55, 57, 60,
  82, 137
 rigging, 24–26, 28, 36–38, 62,
  106–107
 sign of democracy, 131
 stolen votes, 35, 59, 62, 141–142
 straw that broke the camel's back, 67
 women's participation, 57–58
Kadivar, Mohsen, 30–32, 83–84, 91,
 101, 148
Kadkhodai, Abbas Ali, 33–34
Kahrizak detention center, 82, 113
kangaroo courts, 41, 83, 85, 133, 136,
 144
Karroubi, Mehdi
 charges against Islamic Republic,
  82–83, 87, 90–91
 demonstrations, calling for, 35
 economic and social platform, 110
 June 2009 election, questioning
  results of, 23, 35
 as reformist, 56, 100, 117
 revolutionary leader, 26, 118,
  138, 144
 rotating leadership, 147
 supporters, 105–106
 Žižek preferring Mousavi over, 119
Khalil Sakkakini Cultural Center,
 153–154
Khamenei, Sayyid Ali
 in BBC report, 34
 butt of joke, 81
 crackdown, 109
 discredited by Ahmadinejad, 57
 disregarding facts, 144
 government as illegitimate, 100
 June 2009 presidential election, loser
  of, 60–61
 military strikes prompting nuclear
  expansion, 129–130
Khatami, Mohammad
 campaigning for Mousavi, 58, 62
 presidency of, 29, 37, 56–57, 64–65,
  106–107
 recount of June 2009 election, calling
  for, 33
 as reformist, 37, 57, 64, 68, 100
 revolutionary leader, 25–26, 118,
  138, 144

Khatami, Mohammad (*continued*)
 rotating leadership, 147
Khomeini, Ruhollah
 28-Mordadism, 75–77
 American Hostage Crisis, exploiting,
  124–125
 death and funeral, 56–57, 145
 George Soros, ridiculing, 131
 Iran-Iraq (1980-1988) war,
  prolonging, 79, 124
 revolutionary leader, 147
 theocracy, establishing, 124–125
 Velayat-e Faqih, 75–76, 117
King, Jr., Martin Luther (MLK), 26, 29,
 65–66, 73, 139–141, 148
Kittrie, Orde, 130–131, 136–137
Kuwait, 79, 124

Lapham, Lewis, 133–134
Lebanon
 elections, 54–55, 109
 Hezbollah, 43–44, 54, 79, 109
 Israeli invasion, 79–80, 86
 Nasrallah, Seyyed Hassan, 35, 44,
  63–64, 109
 refugee camps, 103, 155, 157–158
the Left
 Iranian, 46, 76, 98, 103, 110, 112, 114
 Western, 97–99, 104, 106, 113–114,
  120–121, 141
Leverett, Flint and Hillary
 defense of Ahmadinejad
  government, 141–144
 neoconservatives connection,
  142, 145
 orientalist fools, 146, 148
 questions of, 147
 as racists, 149–150
Levy, Gideon, 34–35, 43
Littin, Miguel, 154

Mahdavi, Pardis, 58–59
Majidi, Majid, 57–58
Majlis, 26
Makhmalbaf, Mohsen, 28, 50, 57, 81,
 83, 101
Makhmalbaf, Samira, 50
Malcolm X, 51, 65, 73, 148
Maloney, Suzanne, 130, 136
Mandela, Nelson, 26, 29
Marx, Karl, 45, 106, 119

Masters and Masterpieces of Iranian Cinema (Dabashi), 46
McCain, John, 56, 99
media, 41, 47–49, 98, 100–102, 114, 127
See also television
Mehdi's Army, 43–44
middle class, 56, 103, 105–111, 114
Middle East, 39, 43–44, 54, 85, 97
Middle East Media Research Institute (MEMRI), 132
Milani, Abbas, 128–132, 134–137, 143
military strikes
backfiring, 41
creating conditions for coup, 140
Israel threatening, 53, 55, 98, 131
Milani proposals, 129–130, 133–136, 143
neoconservatives wish for, 142, 145
nuclear stalemate, 44
Moezzi, Melody, 51
Mohajerani, Ata, 34, 83, 101
Mohtashami, Ali Akbar, 33
Mojahedin-e Khalq Organization, 76, 84, 139, 144
monarchists, 63, 68, 70, 132, 139, 144, 157
Monroe, Marilyn, 120
Montazeri, Hussein-Ali, 38–39, 68, 84, 91, 100, 146–147
Mortazavi, Said, 146
Mousavi, Mir Hossein
AbuKhalil, critiqued by, 102
Ahmadinejad, calling for resignation of, 148
artists as supporters, 57–58
awareness of flaws, 65
campaign, 61–62
credentials, 57, 62
Dabashi's preference for, 29, 119
December 30, 2009 demonstrations, 162
economic and social platform, 56–57, 62, 110–111
flawed assessment of, 118
green color adoption, 28, 52, 58, 65, 67, 114–115
June 2009 election, questioning results of, 23, 33
leadership
civil rights movement, as part of, 25, 84

Mousavi, Mir Hossein (*continued*)
Green Movement leader, 25–26, 78–80
Iran-Iraq (1980-1988) war, 11, 25, 38, 62
as reformist, 25, 37, 56, 58, 100, 110
revolutionary leader, 100, 117, 144
rotating leadership, 147
uprising, representative of, 88
middle class favoring, 56, 114
MLK and Nelson Mandela, compared to, 26, 29, 65–66
objectives, 148
Rahnavard, Zahra (spouse), 25, 38, 57–58, 62, 112
rallies, calling for, 35
supporters, 24–26, 28, 36–38, 105–108, 110–111, 114–115
Žižek's preference for, 119
Muharram, 145–146
Mute Dreams, Blind Owls, and Dispersed Knowledges (Fischer), 53

9/11
28-Mordad, compared to, 73
Afghan and Iraq invasions, leading to, 67, 80, 86, 124
apocalyptic vision, 51
CIA incompetence, 149
Iranian candlelight vigil, 37
Islamophobia, 32, 95
Naderi, Amir, 74
Nafisi, Azar, 58–59, 128
Najafi, Shahin, 68, 101
Naji al-Ali, 154–158
Nasrallah, Seyyed Hassan, 35, 44, 63–64, 109
Neda, 50–51, 65, 83, 87, 125–127, 140
neoconservatives
condescension of, 113
Iran Democracy Project, 24 132, 134–136
Leveretts' dealing with, 142, 144–145
plots against Iran, 128, 142
threat to Green Movement, 80
Neshat, Shirin, 45–47
Netanyahu, Benjamin, 35, 54, 59–60
New York Times, 101–102, 109, 111–112, 124, 141

nonviolence
    civil disobedience, 25–26, 29, 69,
        112, 140
    civil rights movement, 65, 70, 84,
        86, 123, 139–140
    denunciation of violence, 82–84
    during June 2009 election, 33
    during rallies, 35–36
    velvet coup, 131
nuclear Iran, 40–41, 44, 129–130, 137

Obama, Barak
    Cairo speech, 54, 116, 137
    campaign as Internet-savvy, 56
    CIA, angry with, 149
    diplomacy, 41, 136, 145
    Iranian civil rights, support for, 40,
        138–139
    Islamophobia, 95
    Middle East peace process, 44
    no change from Bush, 59, 98
    not engaging Ahmadinejad
        government, 144
    Rosa Parks, connection to, 140
Obama, Michelle, 57, 139
opposition movement. *See also* protests
    belittled, 147
    covert support, 137
    crackdowns on, 124, 138, 140
    expatriates, 87, 93, 139, 144, 146
    growing, 88
    middle class contingent, 105–108
    Milani's role in, 128, 130–132
    MKO, 68, 70
Osama bin Laden, 52, 124

Pahlavi, Reza, 30, 84, 132, 139
Pahlavi regime, 74, 89, 132
Pakistan, 66, 98, 124, 140, 149
Palestine
    Azmi Bishara as leading intellectual,
        104
    cinema, 103, 153–154
    Gaza massacre, 86
    Hamas, 43–44
    Hanzala, hero of, 154–158
    Iranian solidarity, 63, 109
    Islamic Republic presence in, 79
    Israeli terrorism, 83
    Naji al-Ali, native son, 154–155, 157
    refugee camps, 103, 157–158

Palestine (*continued*)
    Zionist land grab, 116
Palfrey, John, 132
Palin, Sarah, 125–127
Parks, Rosa, 65, 140, 148
parliament of Iran, 26, 39, 45, 55, 76,
        100, 102
Pasdaran, 32–33, 70, 107–108, 138
poetry, 60, 69, 73–74, 93
the poor
    Ahmadinejad government subsidies,
        61, 108, 114, 116
    poverty as Rafsanjani legacy, 57
    support for Ahmadinejad, 25, 56, 105,
        110, 116–117
Powell, Colin, 95
presidential election of 1997, 37, 50,
        56–57, 64
propaganda
    American journalists as tools of,
        127
    Baha'i fears of accusation, 94
    December 30, 2009 demonstrations,
        161–163
    Israeli, 55, 99
    Leveretts fooled by, 145–146
    national television used for, 27
    opponents as CIA agents, 144
    Republican Propaganda Mill,
        133–134
protests. *See also* opposition movement
    Freudian analysis of, 117–118
    Hanzala watching over, 158
    June 2009 election spurring, 23, 35
    nonviolent, 100
    Saudi/US involvement, 99
    staged, 102
    thorn and thistle chant, 33
    Žižek's analysis of, 115, 117

Qur'an, 131

racism
    civil rights movement transcending,
        86
    Iranian security forces viewed as
        Arabs, 157–158
    Israeli, 54, 59, 109
    Leveretts facing possible charge,
        149–150
    racial profiling, 95

racism (*continued*)
El-Sherbini, Marwa Ali, murder of, 126
Western racist policies, 108
Raed (Palestinian filmmaker), 154
Rafsanjani, Ali Akbar Hashemi, 56–57, 107–108
Rahnavard, Zahra, 25, 38, 57–58, 62, 112
Rahnema, Saeed, 98
Ram, Haggai, 55
Ramallah, 153
Rasul Akram Hospital, 26–27
Reading Lolita in Tehran (Nafisi), 25, 58–59, 113
Reagan administration, 51, 79, 124
Reform Movement
28-Mordadism, 77
arrests, 27–28, 83
goals of, 93
June 2009 election, response to, 26
middle class involvement, 105
Milani connection, 132
Public Prosecutor's indictment, 75
reformist contingent in BBC, 34
reformist leaders
Abtahi, 27
Hajjarian, 27–28, 83
Karroubi, 56, 100, 117
Khatami, 37, 57, 64, 68, 100
Mousavi, 25, 37, 56, 58, 100, 110
treason charge, 94
trials, 128, 131–136
velvet revolution plot, 81
refugee camps, 103, 155, 157–158
Revolution of 1977-1979
Chelkowski/Dabashi archive, 161–162
different from civil rights movement, 66, 112
form of closure, 74–75
Foucault on, 113, 115
Islamization of, 45, 78, 89, 118
Khomeini and, 124, 147
reaction to monarchial tyranny, 79
returning to roots, 115
slogan, 87
traumatic memories, causing, 65
Žižek's musings on, 52
Reza'i, Mohsen, 23, 56, 106, 110
Robin, Michael, 130, 136

Rohrabacher, Dana, 130, 137
Roosevelt, Kermit, 132, 143
Ruholamini, Mohsen, 87
Rumi, 60, 94
rural population, 56, 111–112

Sadjapour, Karim, 130, 136
Sadr, Shadi, 83
Sakkakini Foundation, 153–154
Salehi-Isfahani, Djavad, 106, 111
Sales, Mehdi Akhavan, 73–74
sanctions
Milani encouraging, 129–131, 134–137, 143
threats of, 24, 41, 44, 53, 63, 70, 98
US in favor of, 133–134, 136–140, 142, 145
Sane'i, Yousef, 84, 91
Sartre, Jean-Paul, 103, 120
Saudis, 98–103, 124
Schmitt, Karl, 134
second generation Iranians, 114, 117
secularism, 89, 110, 112, 114, 132
security forces
Basiji and *Pasdaran*, 107–108, 138
brutal and violent, 80, 82–83, 89, 92, 100, 145, 150, 157
police dispersing demonstrations, 34–35
as rapists, 87, 90–92, 126, 144–145
Revolutionary Guards, 32–33, 116, 149
Sepah-e Mohammad Rasul Allab, 28
Sexual Politics in Modern Iran (Afari), 112
Shahbazi, Parviz, 50
Shah of Iran, 38, 65, 75–77, 162
Shajarian, Mohammad Reza, 27
Shams, Fatemeh, 93
Sharpe, Gene, 131
al-Sherbini, Marwa Ali, 102, 126–127
Shibli, Adania, 154
Shi'i
clerics, 63, 82, 84–85, 91
fate of Shi'i Lebanese, 63
intra-Shi'i sectarianism, 94
jurists, 31–32, 110
legitimacy issues, 45
Neda Aqa Soltan as female representative, 50
Shiraz University, 27, 35

Aqa Soltan, Neda, 50–51, 65, 83, 87,
  125–127, 140
Soltanpour, Said, 158
Soros, George, 131, 135
Soroush, Abdokarim, 83, 100–101
Soviet Union, 51, 104, 124
Staging a Revolution (Chelkowski;
  Dabashi), 161–162

28-Mordadism, 73–77
Taliban, 66, 79, 91, 124
Tehran University, 27, 34–35, 75–76,
  121
television
  airing pro-Ahmadinejad rallies, 33, 37,
    110, 146, 162
  broadcasting patriotic songs, 27
  kangaroo court sessions aired, 83–84,
    100. 133
  rally at national headquarters, 28
theocracy
  brutality of, 85, 92, 124–125, 144
  democratic, 55
  fragility of, 39, 76
  legacy, 61
  middle class uprising, 110
  revolution, resisting notion, 150
  theocratic dictatorship, 66
  thinly disguised, 79
Theology of Discontent (Dabashi),
  45–46
Twitter, 33–34, 40, 57, 64, 66–67. *See
  also* Internet

unemployment, 25, 38, 61, 106–107,
  111
United States. *See also* 9/11
  Afghanistan, presence in, 54, 59, 80,
    85–86, 98, 124, 133, 150
  American Hostage Crisis, 67, 76–77,
    79, 118, 123–125, 146
  American Israel Public Affairs
    Committee (AIPAC), 62–64
  American punditry, 141–142,
    149–150
  CIA, 98–103, 106, 132, 144, 149
  Civil Rights Movement, 148
  House Foreign Affairs Committee
    hearing, 127–131, 133–136, 138
  Iraq occupation, 54, 59, 80, 85, 115,
    124

United States. (*continued*)
  Islamophobia, 32, 88, 95–96
  June 2009 elections, recognizing
    results, 28
  nuclear Iran, concerns over, 40–41, 44,
    129–130, 137
  sanctions
    favoring, 133–134, 136–140, 142,
      145
    Milani encouraging, 129–131,
      134–137, 143
    threats of, 24, 41, 44, 53, 63, 98
  United States Agency for International
    Development (USAID), 139
university system, 106–107, 111

Vali Faqih, 24, 26, 60, 76
Velayat-e Faqih
  Kadivar, 148
  Khomeini, 75, 117
  rejection of, 70, 116
  religious fascism, 83
  undemocratic, 56
velvet coup, 128, 131–132, 135
velvet revolution, 37, 81, 106, 113
violence. *See also* Neda Aqa Soltan;
    security forces
  absolutism, 79
  civil rights movement, violent
    dimensions of, 66
  distorting political culture, 85, 88–89
  impatience, 68
  legacy of US invasions, 91, 124
  Max Weber on, 82
  against the media, 118
  Obama's reaction, 40–41
  obedience, as means of gaining, 92
  post-electoral, 113, 125
  pressing on despite, 63, 92–93
  ruining image of Islam, 90–92
  silencing dissenters with, 32
  ungodly, 136
voting
  80% turnout in June 2009 elections, 24,
    38, 60, 63
  chants and slogans, 35, 69
  June 2009 election as rigged, 24–26,
    28, 36–38, 106–107
  on next phase of Islamic Republic, 70
  not proving legitimacy of Islamic
    Republic, 146

voting (*continued*)
    stolen votes of June 2009 election, 35, 59, 62, 141–142

war on terror, 52, 98, 133–134
Weber, Max, 82, 113, 119
Wolfowitz, Paul, 62–63, 98
women
    demonstration participants, 25, 57–58, 106, 110–111, 150
    lipstick jihadis, 25, 58–59
    Mousavi supporters, 56
    rape, 87, 126, 144–145
    women's rights, 37, 41, 57–58, 64–65, 70, 100–101

Yazdi, Mesbah, 26, 31
youth culture. *See also* Internet
    artists, 47
    candlelight vigil for 9/11, 37
    chants, 125
    middle class, 105–106, 111, 114
    Neda Aqa Soltan as icon, 50–51
    sanctions hurting, 44, 139
    third path, 93
You Tube, 66, 68. *See also* Internet

Zionists, 58–60, 82–83, 85–86, 91, 116, 131
Žižek, Slavoj, 52, 97, 103, 113–121